Enjoy

California! by *Camaro*

The great food and wine adventure (at low cost)

- Hidden Restaurants: Northern California
- Hidden Restaurants: Southern California
- Little Restaurants of San Francisco
- Little Restaurants of Los Angeles
- Little Restaurants of San Diego
- Wine Tasting in California: A Free Weekend
- L. A. On Foot: A Free Afternoon

Perhaps the most beautifully illustrated books in the Western World. Glove compartment size, and only $1.95.

At your favorite bookstore, or by mail from the publisher. See back of book for order information.

★★★★★ A Camaro Five Star Guide

The Little Restaurants of San Diego

by Lanny Wagstaff

Illustrations by David Yeadon

Camaro Publishing Co.
LOS ANGELES–SAN FRANCISCO

Illustrations on pages 13, 23, 61, 69, 79, 95, and 103 are by Shirley Richards.

ISBN 0-913290-07-6

Copyright © 1973, 1974 Camaro Publishing Co.
All Rights Reserved
Printed in the United States

CAMARO PUBLISHING COMPANY
LOS ANGELES, CALIFORNIA 90009

4567890987654

Contents

Introduction	7

AMERICAN
- College Restaurant — 10
- Hob Nob Hill — 12

BEEF
- First Edition — 14
- Kelly's — 16
- Pinnacle Peak — 18
- Saska's — 20
- John Bull — 22

CHINESE
- China Land — 24
- New Moon — 26

CONTINENTAL
- Thee Bungalow — 28
- Greenery — 30

CREPES, OMELETTES
- Crepe Shop — 32

FILIPINO
- Lourdes — 34
- Sampaquita — 36

FRENCH
- Cafe Lautrec — 38

GERMAN
- Black Forest Inn — 40
- Bratskellar — 42
- Schnitzelbank — 44

HEALTH
- Gatekeeper — 46
- Prophet — 48

ITALIAN
- DeAngelis — 50
- Giulio's — 52
- Nicolosi's — 54
- Venice — 56
- Zolezzi's — 58
- Old Spaghetti Factory — 60

JAPANESE
- Miki-San — 62

KOSHER
- Blumer's Bakery — 64

LEBANESE
- Antoine's Sheik — 66

MEXICAN
- Alfonso's Hideaway — 68
- Aljones — 70
- Bea's Rancho Chico — 72
- El Juan's Cafe — 74
- Rosendo's Hideaway — 76

POLISH
- Three Mermaids — 78

SEAFOOD
- Tom Lai's — 80
- Fishermen's Wharf Grotto — 82

Fish Place	84
Krishna Mulvaney	86
Ocean Fresh Seafood Cafe	88
World Famous	90

SMORGASBORD

Nordic Inn	92

SPANISH

Restaurant Madrid	94

SPLURGE

Anthony's Star of the Sea	96
Aspen Mine Co.	98
Chart House	100
Chez Francois	102
Lubach's	104
Old Trieste	106
Botsford's Old Place	108

LUNCH

East San Diego	110
Hillcrest & Balboa Park	111
Old Town	112
Downtown	113
Southeast San Diego	114
The Beaches	115
Coronado	116

SPECIALTY FOOD SHOPS	117
RESTAURANTS BY REGION	123
ALPHABETICAL INDEX	125
AFTER HOURS	127
READER REPLY	131

Introduction

There are many excellent little restaurants hidden throughout San Diego—a few off busy Mission Blvd., some near Balboa Park, a couple around San Diego Bay, and even one on the second floor of a furniture store building. At any of these places exciting foods, to be eaten with fingers, chopsticks, or even forks, await those willing to venture forth to these out-of-the-way, and often times, exotic places.

Finding these restaurants on your own isn't easy. It's risky enough getting good food at the places you already know about much less exploring unknown new ones. Fortunately, good food does exist in town—and at low prices. To find it you just have to know where to go.

Researching *The Little Restaurants of San Diego* carried us to all corners of the city to try everyplace worthy of mention where excellent food and low prices are in happy concord. After a year and a half of searching, we narrowed our list down to the 50 or so presented here, and each is highly recommended—sometimes for atmosphere but mostly for great food. Any deficiencies we noted are covered along with their redeeming features.

Because dining out is a special occasion, the restaurant you choose—whether an old friend or a new place with the best of recommendations—should provide a good meal. To do that the restaurant should have a pleasant look about it, the service should be efficient if not friendly, and the food should be well prepared.

The most important ingredient, of course, is the food. It is easy to endure ordinary service in ordinary surroundings if the food is a bit extraordinary. There is very little a magnificent view or sparkling service can do to rescue mediocre food.

We find good food easy enough to recognize. It tastes good. It always seems to have sufficient flavor to keep the tongue interested throughout the meal and, in memory, linger on into the next day. We have also found that good food has the remarkable power to lift one out of the depression of the day, soothe angered sensibilities, or momentarily brighten the gloomiest of prospects.

Good food need not be expensive. If the meal has been delicious and the service delightful, there is seldom any resentment when the bill is delivered. On the other hand, poor food and mean service is too expensive at any price.

For that very special night when you have allocated a few extra dollars for dining out, we have listed a few splurges. Two of these are among the standard local restaurants for an evening of celebration. If you prefer less splendor and more food, we have included the two current favorites from the beef and shellfish houses around town. Since these can be quite busy some nights of the week, we have also noted other places where good food can be eaten in less hectic surroundings.

In addition to these splurges, there are scores of small lunch spots around the city worthy of mention. Because most people eat near where they work, some of the best of these places go unrecognized except by a few. We have listed every good one we knew about or could find. Some others, no doubt, eluded us—but not many, and these we'll leave to be discovered later in future editions.

No one interested in the pursuit of good-tasting food stops the search with restaurants. Bakeries, delicatessens, and tortillarias all offer delicious snacks or essential ingredients. To help you in this search, my wife, Karen, has been studying the food shops while we were out looking for little restaurants. She found places to buy tofu, handmade tortillas, homemade sausage, and rolls shaped like turtles. Hopefully, these specialty gourmet shops will help put even more good food into your life and tummy.

Lanny Wagstaff

ABOUT THE AUTHOR

A native San Diegan and San Diego State graduate, Lanny Wagstaff has discovered that paying high prices doesn't necessarily buy good food. Good food and service comes from caring about what is served along with caring about the tummies of the customers, more than just mere profits. With this thought in mind Lanny educated his palate by visiting nearly every restaurant in town, and devouring hundreds maybe even thousands of meals—some good and some not so. The best of Lanny's extensive search for little restaurants are presented to you here. Lanny is now dieting, fixing up an old house, and otherwise enjoying the life of an inflation-fighting *bon vivant*.

ACKNOWLEDGEMENTS

For their help in preparing this book, there are almost too many mouths to thank. Lynn's, Pete's, and Barbara's were foremost; with great docility they ate anything the occasion required. Bob I must thank for knowing so many good places; Dave, for knowing all the worst places, save two gems which were included; Pete, again, for his time and resources; and Karen, herself, who persevered, nearly outgrowing an entire wardrobe.

Note: All restaurants serve at least beer or wine unless specified otherwise.

College Restaurant

In the big city, family-style restaurants are about as plentiful as passenger pigeons. Only by virtue of irrepressible enthusiasm for their work, inexplicable love for their fellow man, or sheer inertia, are the owners disposed to keep the doors open. Out in the country, some are hanging on. But in the city—at least this city—they are no longer an endangered species. They are extinct.

The next best thing may be the College Restaurant. It is a home-style building that should have a nice green lawn and a big oak tree or two shading it. Instead it is curb-to-front-door in asphalt, which makes for convenient parking.

The interior features a counter, padded booths, and carpeting rather than tables and hardwood floors, but the home cooking is there. Chicken, meat loaf, chicken casserole, inexpensive steaks, and the like are served by friendly women, some of whom look as long-established as the restaurant.

The chicken is good, too: three pieces fried to the traditional golden brown, served with potatoes, good corn fritters and honey, and corn pone. Preceding all that is a choice of soup or salad. If the price of chicken stays within reason, the place may well continue charging $2.15 for the dinner.

6695 El Cajon Blvd., San Diego. (714) 469-1140
Daily: 6 a.m. - 8:30 p.m.
No reservations
No alcoholic beverages
No credit cards

THE Best ANYWHERE!
CHICKEN • STEAKS
ROASTS • SEA FOOD
OPEN 6AM • CLOSE 8:30PM

montezuma
0 ½ mi
College
el cajon
rolando
university
college

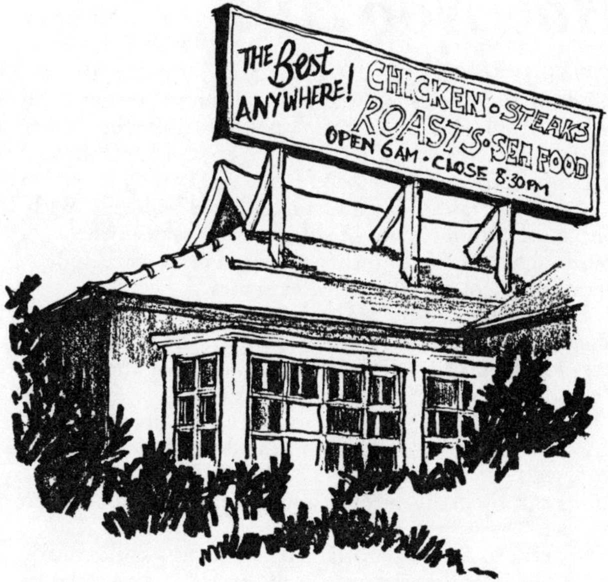

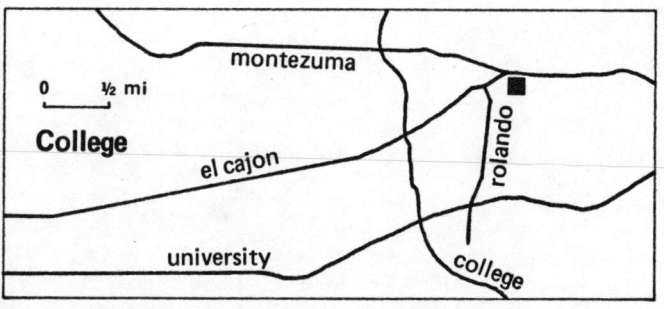

Hob Nob Hill

What is American food? It is country-fried steak, chicken and dumplings, breaded veal cutlet, liver and onions, and turkey. The Hob Nob extends the list even further, offering regular daily specials of leg of lamb, corned beef, short ribs, roast pork, fried chicken, and ham.

The restaurant bakes all its own bread and rolls. With each meal a mini-loaf of bread is served: white, wheat, sourdough, or raisin. Freshly prepared desserts include German chocolate cake and cream pies.

Each entree can be ordered as part of a full dinner (soup, salad, dessert, and coffee) or *a la carte.* The latter already includes the bread, vegetable, and potato for about $3. A small dinner salad is a few pennies extra.

What is most impressive about this restaurant is the service. Each party is greeted at the door by the owner-host, who shows them to the best available table and then points out the daily specials and the entrees of particular interest. The waitresses are efficient and pleasant. The little extra touches—such as being brought a chilled fork for the salad and a warmed spoon for the soup—made us feel as though we were eating at one of the most elegant restaurants in town. No alcoholic beverages are served.

2271 First Ave., San Diego. (714) 239-8176
Sun. - Fri. 7 a.m. - 8 p.m.; closed Sat.
AE, BA, MC

Little Restaurants of San Diego / 13

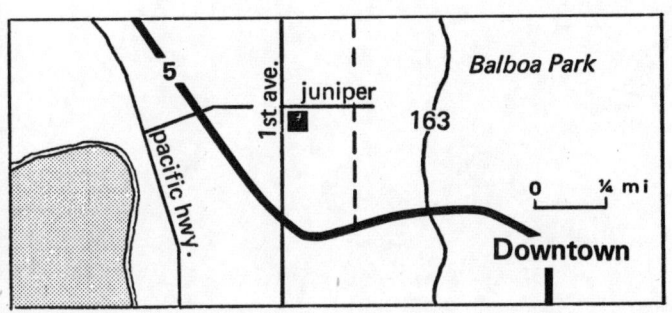

The First Edition

The First Edition now offers a prime-rib dinner for under $5. The price is good from 5:30 to 7:30 any night of the week. As with the more expensive version later in the evening, it comes with salad and bread only. A potato is extra.

The onion soup is excellent, served with thick melted cheese over the top. It makes a fine snack if you are not hungry enough for the prime rib or if you want to share the dinner. For that matter, on any cold, damp night, especially late in the evening when you happen to be in the mood for a bite to eat, this soup would be ideal.

Needless to say, reservations are not necessary when dining between 5 and 7 on Monday evening. Dress is semi-casual.

The First Edition is located on the second floor of a furniture store building across Highway 8 from the Mission Valley shopping center.

If you leave the house too late for the special, or should it be discontinued, try Sexton's Steak House on El Cajon Blvd. During the entire evening it is full of people, all happy to be eating prime rib at a bargain price.

1299 Camino Del Rio South, San Diego. (714) 291-2400
Tues. - Sat. 11:30 - 2, 5 - 12; Sun. & Mon. 5 - 10
AE, BA, CB, MC

Little Restaurants of San Diego / 15

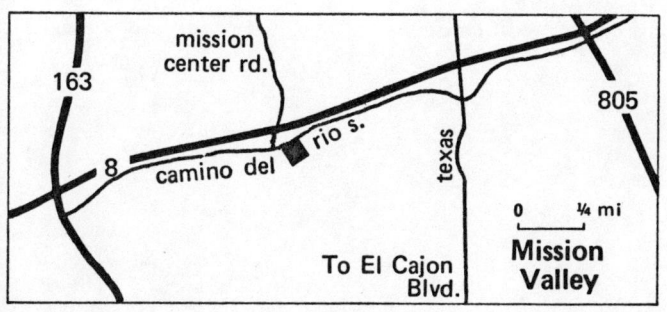

ID
Kelly's

The favorite steak house of those who like their steaks big, good, and inexpensive is Kelly's. Its menu is very limited: steak, lobster, and prime rib in a total of eight offerings. The most popular is the Chateaubriand for two. Served with a salad, garlic bread, a potato, and a tenth of champagne, it will cost you around $10. However, if you arrive and order before 6:30, it is a dollar or so less—still for two. The piece of meat is huge, plenty for two or even three people.

The London broil sells for about half that price at any time of the day. The menu suggests that the Chateaubriand will have a better flavor. Yet, despite the lower price, the London broil has a comparable flavor and seems as large. It can be ordered for two, also, though the menu makes no such offer. All that need be done is to order the broil and the meal service for the other person, which gives you another salad, more bread, and another potato for an extra $1.25.

Reservations are not accepted. On weekends there can be a wait if you arrive at around 6 p.m. Other times and other days, the large dining room should be able to handle your party. The dress is hard to characterize. For many patrons, it seems to be a sort of dressy casual.

248 Hotel Circle Dr., San Diego. (714) 296-2131
Mon. - Fri. 11 a.m. - 11:45 p.m.; Sat. & Sun. 4 - 11:45
No reservations
All major credit cards

Little Restaurants of San Diego / 17

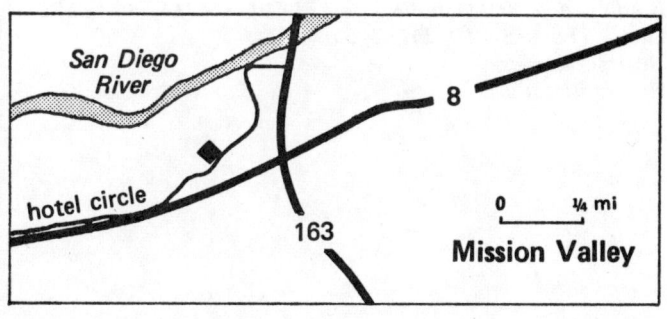

Pinnacle Peak

When the dull clanging of the cowbell is heard throughout the hall, regular patrons of this restaurant begin to grin. They know that somewhere in the darker recesses of the restaurant, an amputation and humiliation is being committed.

Each person seated at the long rows of picnic tables, with gingham oilcloth coverings and metal kerosene lanterns, turns in the direction of the bell. They all watch the cowgirl with the foot-long scissors wind her way through the rows of tables to the man with the puzzled expression and forbidden article.

If that man, who is now sitting there innocently wondering what the stir and excitement is all about, had used his powers of observation earlier, he might have noticed that the walls, ceilings, and fixtures are festooned with ties. And he just might have become suspicious when he observed that there was not a whole tie to be seen—only halves. At the very least, his curiosity should have been piqued by the management's bizarre taste in interior decoration.

In addition to this nightly entertainment Pinnacle Peak has steaks: smaller "cowgirl" and hefty "cowboy" T-bone steaks, thick and surprisingly tender. Cooked over mesquite coals in a huge brazier in the middle of the room, the steaks acquire a zesty outdoor flavor. Either steak comes with a small salad, beans, and bread.

No frills, no expensive prices, no reservations. Just steaks. And if you must wear a tie, remember that we warned you.

Bradley Ave. at Magnolia Ave., El Cajon. (714) 448-8882
Sun. - Thurs. 5 - 10; Fri. & Sat. 5 - 11
No reservations
No credit cards

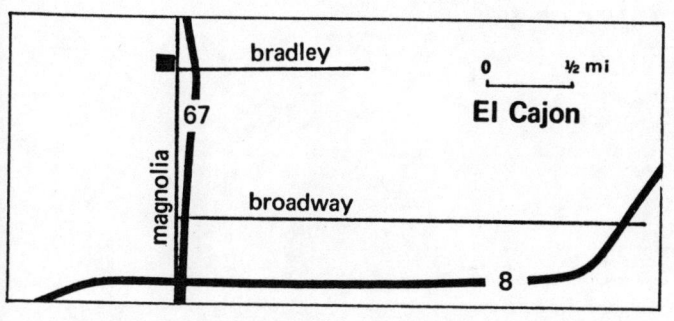

Saska's

Saska's restaurant has been in existence for over 20 years, and for as long as I can remember it has served incredible hamburgers.

The steaks have gone up in price, but until recently the hamburger had not. With french fries or baked potato, it has been selling for around $2. It is a large patty—almost as big as the large bun on which it is served—and over half an inch thick. The meat is ground fresh in the kitchen from steak, so it has a good lean taste and can be ordered less than well done with confidence. The french fries are, alas, no longer cut fresh in the kitchen, but are bought frozen. The baked potatoes are still reliably good.

Actually, the hamburger could be served without any kind of potato and still be almost too much to eat. The dinner salad is also large enough for two. You need only ask for an extra plate. (The Roquefort dressing contains enough garlic to parboil the inside of an unaccustomed mouth.)

Steaks and the rest are always available if a more expensive meal is desired. There's more than one steak on the menu still under $5. The breakfast menu available after midnight offers three eggs, ham, pork chops, or steak, plus potatoes and toast, of course. Any of these offer a delightful late evening snack before a long ride home. Waiters are very friendly and helpful. Dress is casual.

3768 Mission Blvd., San Diego. (714) 488-7311
Daily: 6 p.m. - 3 a.m.
AE, BA, CB, MC

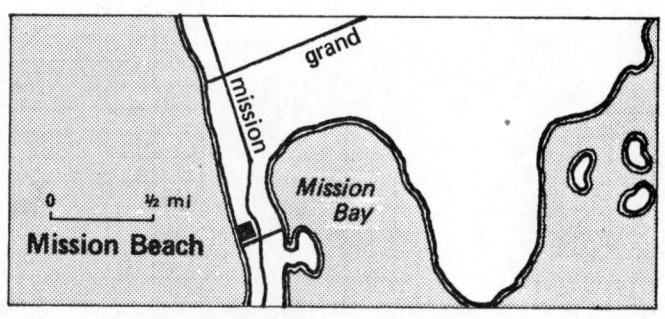

John Bull

Everyone seems to like the John Bull. Perhaps it is the friendliness. Or maybe it is the warm feeling of being in an old English inn. Each of the small dining rooms has a fireplace. The waiters and hostess are in costume. The menu comes on the bone of a bull's shoulder—hardly authentic, but very effective.

The main reason for the John Bull's popularity, however, has to do with the prices: good solid beef dinners for under $5. There are the usual inexpensive brochette, teriyaki, and chopped beef. But there are also steaks and English-cut prime rib at the same low prices. Full prime rib and the various combination plates are more expensive.

All dinners include a walk to the salad bar and warm bread. An artichoke, ear of corn, or baked potato is a little extra. Reservations advisable.

2200 Highland Ave., National City. (714) 474-2201
Sun. 4:30 - 10; Mon. - Thurs. 5:30 - 10:30; Fri. & Sat.
  5:30 - midnight
BA, MC

Little Restaurants of San Diego / 23

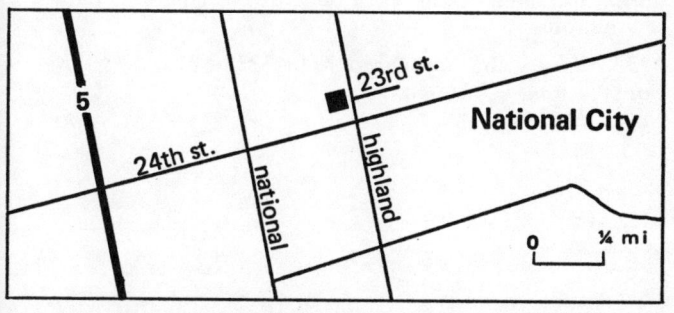

China Land

China Land is not much to look at. From the outside it could pass for a drive-in—a Chinese drive-in of red and gold. In fact, it is. In the center of the building there is a room for car service. If you drive up in front of that room and sit with your lights on, someone will come out and take your order. If you prefer to eat inside, there is a cafe-style bar to the right where parties of one can dine. To the left is the main dining room, which looks like the lair of a dragon lady, again in red and gold.

It's a great place. A number of people recommend it, and for good reason. The food is excellent. The vegetables are fresh, and even when cooked they retain their crispness. The meats are tender. The sauces are outstanding. The sweet-and-sour sauce, for example, is smooth and consistent, never raw or biting. All the food exhibits skill of preparation.

Prices are reasonable. The usual dishes, such as cashew chicken, snow peas, and sweet-and-sour shrimp, have been selling for less than $2 each. The tomato beef is an unusual dish in the same price range: thinly sliced beef in a delicately spiced tomato sauce with tomato quarters and a sprinkling of onions and peppers.

This is a family restaurant, and the dress can be very casual. The waiters seem friendly and helpful. They will gladly offer suggestions to those wishing to order *a la carte*.

No reservations. A few minutes' wait is to be expected during the dinner hour, even on a week night. But only a few minutes.

3135 Midway Dr., San Diego. (714) 233-1255
Daily: 4 p.m. - 3:30 a.m.
No credit cards

Little Restaurants of San Diego / 25

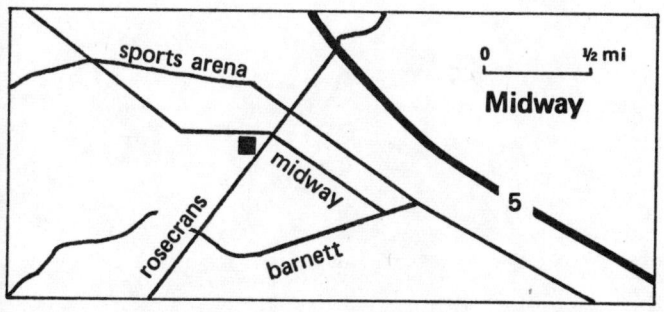

New Moon

I went into Woo Chee Chong's market one day and asked the butcher where the best Chinese food in town was to be found. He said that if I wanted authentic Chinese food I should try the New Moon. That is where the restaurant owners in town go to eat, he added. I am not too sure about that, but the food can be excellent.

Rather than make particular suggestions, I advise that you put yourself in the hands of the waitress-owner (the waiter seems less informative, but you can try). She will recommend a nice combination of dishes. Or she will let you in on any specials available that day. For example, she told us about the homemade Peking egg roll, which is not always available.

One recommendation I will make is that you do not order the dinner. Chow mein is the central dish, and it tastes rather old. There are far better things on the menu than those offered in the tourist dinners.

The prices are slightly higher than those at China Land. But the New Moon does offer some delightful things not available elsewhere.

Reservations are not necessary. Dress is casual. For those who remember the old Upper Cellar, the New Moon occupies the same facilities.

6559 El Cajon Blvd., San Diego. (714) 583-2722
Tues. - Sun. 11:30 - 10; closed Mon.
No credit cards

Little Restaurants of San Diego / 27

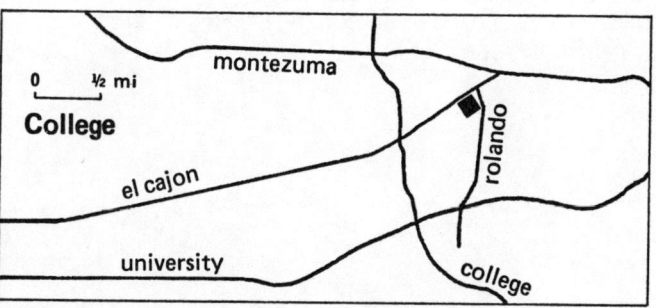

Thee Bungalow

Thee Bungalow is one of the nicest little restaurants around. The owners have managed to convert their old house into a charming place to eat. There are two dining rooms—a large one in the front of the house and a smaller one in the back—and, when the weather isn't inclement, the patio is opened with huge outdoor heaters to ward off the evening chill.

The menu displays a mixture of cuisines which is described as "continental." For example, there is Basque chicken. It is baked in lemon and garlic which permeate the skin, giving the meat a moist texture and a fine lemon flavor.

There is also veal Cordon Bleu which is good. The Jaeger schnitzel is another interesting choice if you are in the mood for veal.

A dish popular among duck fanciers is the orange duck. It will cost more than $5, however. Other possible dinners on the menu include sole amandine and a specialty for the day. The dinner includes a good soup, a salad, and delicious rolls.

This is a very popular restaurant among those who enjoy a nice meal in a pleasant, slightly formal atmosphere. The service is smooth, in keeping with that atmosphere. Because of this, reservations are necessary during the busy dinner hours. Some people like to use the restaurant as an occasion to dress up; others prefer coming in casual clothing.

4996 W. Point Loma Blvd., San Diego. (714) 222-5774
Tues. - Thurs. 5 - 10; Fri. & Sat. 5 - 11; Sun. 5 - 10;
  closed Mon.
BA, MC

8
w. point loma
bacon
sunset cliffs
nimitz
0
¼ mi
Ocean Beach

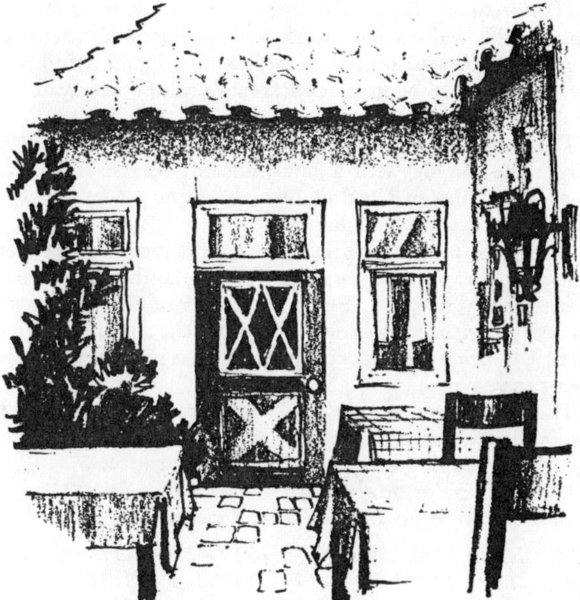

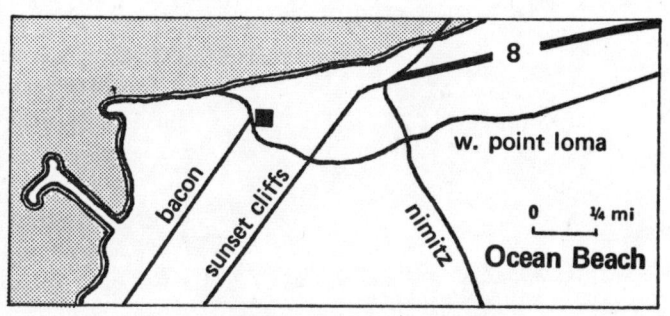

The Greenery

The Greenery is as cool and spacious inside as its name implies. The walls are of stark white plaster, adorned only by nodes of texturing and a large stained-glass window. The booths have been placed casually along the walls, leaving room for plants.

The menu is as seductive as the name and the decor. It tempts the tongue with a small host of treats: steamed vegetables, chicken Cordon Bleu, burgundy beef, beef stroganoff, and rack of lamb.

With such tempting prices we tried them all, but were somewhat disappointed except for the lamb which was, unfortunately over $5. From the looks of the five or six ribs served with each order, however, the lamb was probably worth the price. It is accompanied by a nice mint sauce, most tasty.

The steamed vegetables, however, are inexpensive and good. Cooked neither too much nor too little, they are served with a generous topping of a good hollandaise sauce.

Due to popular demand, there is a wait around the bar on weekends. No reservations. Dress is casual or exotic.

4474 Mission Blvd., San Diego. (714) 276-5831
Mon. - Thurs. 11 - 2, 5 - 11; Fri. 11 - 2, 5 - 11:30;
Sat. 5 - 11:30; Sun. 10 - 2 (brunch), 5 - 10:30
MC

Little Restaurants of San Diego / 31

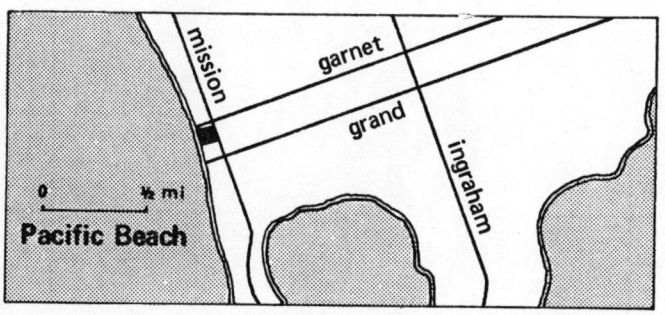

Crepe Shop

As is well known now, a house is not a home, and so is a shop not a restaurant. This is a cafeteria and a post office. During the day, those in line for mail watch those eating and vice versa, while those in line for food watch everyone else.

The decor is more shop than restaurant. There are a few large round tables, but mostly there are simply stools meant to be used at the counter around three walls.

Unlike most restaurants, it offers no wine, and unlike most shops it offers excellent food.

The menu is limited to a few different crepes: stroganoff, curried chicken, shrimp and crab, ham and cheese, and creamed spinach. The stroganoff, while not looking nor tasting quite like a traditional stroganoff, has more flavor than any dish of that name I have ever tried. The creamed spinach is also good-tasting and not heavy or saucey.

The dessert crepes are served with fruit and topped with the cream of your choice (about a dollar each). More fresh fruit would make them better.

The Crepe Shop is the perfect place for a fast dinner. Without wine, a leisurely dinner is impossible, for there is nothing left to do after eating but leave. Perhaps, if enough people request it, the Crepe Shop may be encouraged to add wine to its menu.

3795 Mission Blvd., San Diego. (714) 488-9442
Sun. - Thurs. 8:30 a.m. - 10 p.m.;
  Fri. & Sat. 8:30 a.m. - 11 p.m.
No credit cards

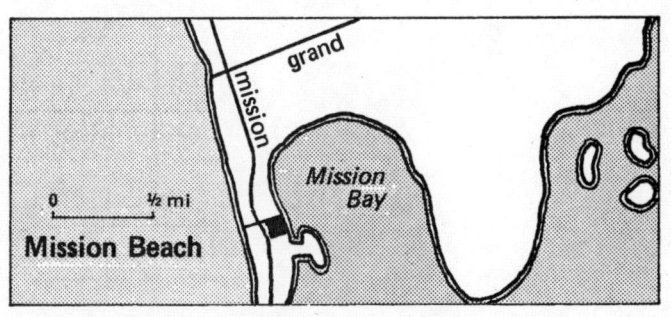

Lourdes

It is nice to have a Filipino restaurant within the city limits, though I would not want to say that it serves the best Filipino food. However, the food is good, filling, and you'll enjoy the change of pace.

This Lourdes, related to the one in National City, is a giant place large enough to feed President Marcos's army, though a bit short on tables and chairs. To contribute a sense of the tropics to all that empty space, paper palm trees have been taped to the ends of the counters. Perhaps the paneled walls and carpeted floor are meant to accompany the American half of the menu.

Exactly why the ceiling was painted orange remains something of a mystery. Since the food is freshly cooked to order, you will have adequate time to formulate your own theories about that ceiling. It must be remembered, however, that a glass of strong San Miguel beer will not make your thinking any clearer.

The menu is similar to Sampaquita's, and the same suggestions about what and how to order are valid at Lourdes. Price are similar, as well.

3804 Rosecrans Ave., San Diego. (714) 296-0443
Tues. - Sun. 11 a.m. - midnight; closed Mon.
BA

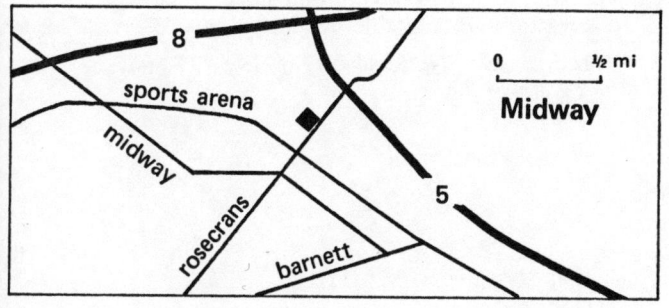

Sampaquita

It may be a few extra minutes' drive to Sampaquita, but it will be worth every minute of it. The restaurant is a family operation. The wife cooks, the daughter waits on the few booths, the son washes the dishes, and the husband supervises. Going into their restaurant is like visiting a happy family in their home, for when they are not busy they are unobtrusively watching television in the back booth. The interior is immaculate, the atmosphere is friendly, and the food is excellent.

Not knowing what to order, we had the waitress bring out Mother to offer a few suggestions. The same procedure would be advisable for anyone else unaccustomed to Filipino food, though noting the dishes we tried may help. Each dish costs about $2.

The food is remarkably like Chinese food, yet with enough differences to make it a unique experience. One orders various dishes and then shares them around the table. So for a party of four there will be great variety, though less quantity of any particular dish.

The fried rice is the best I have had since traveling in the Orient. Inihaw, a sort of fried roast pork, is spectacular. A noodle dish, pansit Canton, was also a delightful surprise. It consists of long, thin, spaghetti-type noodles coated with a sauce that tastes like vaguely soy sauce, only better, into which are added bits of meat and vegetables. Other recommendations are the combination gulay (boiled vegetables with meat), sarciado (fried fish with soy sauce and vegetables), chicken adobo, and sweet-and-sour pork.

Reservations are available but not needed. Dress is casual.

819 National Ave., National City. (714) 477-1065
Daily: 11 a.m. - 2 a.m.
BA

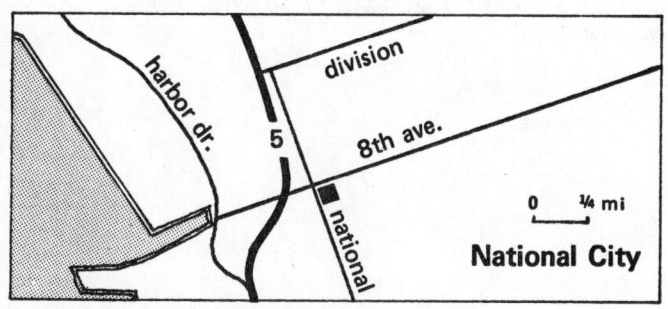

Café Lautrec

The Cafe Lautrec offers a pleasant place to dine. The restaurant is located at the end of a high narrow passageway between two buildings, which gives its patio dining area the effect of a sidewalk cafe. Inside, the windows offer nothing more than plenty of natural light, at least during daylight saving time. The tables are simply, though tastefully, set. The waiter and waitress are friendly and helpful.

There is no set menu. Entrees are changed occasionally, but they remain in the $3 to $5 price range. Each meal is preceded by soup and salad. The soups offered are onion and split pea. Both are good, but the onion is the better of the two. The salad comes as a surprise, for it includes not only lettuce and tomato but bits of other things like cucumber, cheese, and ham. The house dressing is particularly good, and so is the blue cheese. A basket of warm French bread accompanies the meal.

Were the entrees as carefully presented as the table settings, the decor, and the rest of the dinner, this would be a very special place indeed. However, the entrees seem to suffer from early preparation and last-minute warming. As a result, they taste a little old—a serious flaw in some dishes. Cafe Lautrec is too nice not to try, however. And it is currently offering the only reasonably priced French food in the city.

Reservations are not necessary. Dress can be casual or more dressy, if you prefer.

7644 Girard Ave., La Jolla. (714) 459-7577
Mon. 11:30 - 4:30; Tues. - Sat. 11:30 - 9; closed Sun.
No credit cards

Little Restaurants of San Diego / 39

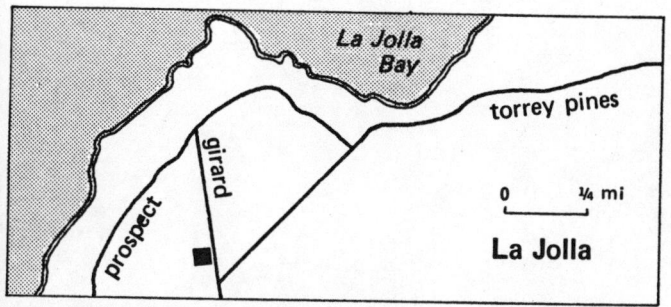

Black Forest Inn

If there is a connection between German food and a Weight Watcher's diet, it would seem to be in the need for the one after eating too much of the other. At the Black Forest there is a different sort of connection, as well.

There are two menus: one for those who do, and another for those who do not. In the food of one go all the forbidden enlargers denied to those on the program. For the latter, the food is inspected, weighed, and kept perfectly "legal."

Ordering from the right side of the menu is simple, but it can be a problem keeping the salad bars straight. To prevent crossovers or confusion, the waitress keeps a stern eye on every move you make toward a salad dressing. When serving the food, however, she can be very pleasant.

The food is well prepared, too; but as in other German restaurants it seems to have been cooked in the afternoon for the evening meal, and does not always taste as fresh as it could.

Reservations are not necessary. Dress is casual.

1037 University Ave., San Diego. (714) 298-2269
Tues. - Fri. 11 - 2, 5 - 9; Sat. 5 - 9; closed Sun. & Mon.
BA

Little Restaurants of San Diego / 41

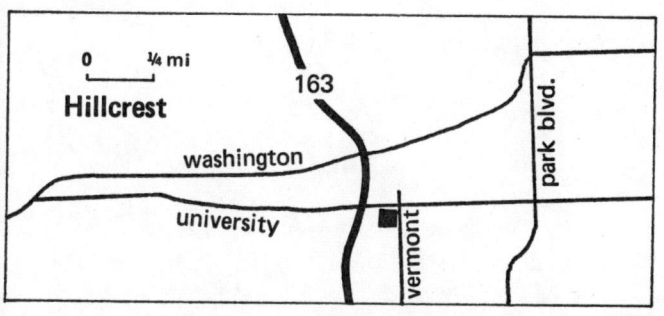

Bratskellar

This is a restaurant good for snacks in all seasons. On a clear day there is a fine view of the cove from the back room. On a cold winter's day there is a fire burning in the main room. (There is a fire on a hot summer's day also, if that appeals to you.) And on any warm day there is a patio out front with tables and umbrellas.

The menu offers equal variety but emphasizes sandwiches, roast beef, corned beef, hamburger, and bratwurst. More expensive, though still less than $4, is the shrimp boiled in beer. It sounds terrible but tastes very good.

For that occasional hot day when the mere thought of food puts beads of perspiration on the forehead, this is one of the few places where a fruit-and-cheese plate can be ordered. Like most good things it is a little complicated. To get the fruit (an apple), you must order the fruit-and-cheese dessert. In order to get sufficient bread and cheese for two, you must order the bread-and-cheese plate.

A bottle of cool white wine will put that kind of light meal in proper perspective, and if you are fortunate you may even have a view. There are no reservations. Dress "as you are."

1250 Prospect St., La Jolla. (714) 454-4244
Mon. - Sat. 11:30 a.m. - 2 a.m.; Sun. 11:30 a.m. - midnight
AE, BA, MC

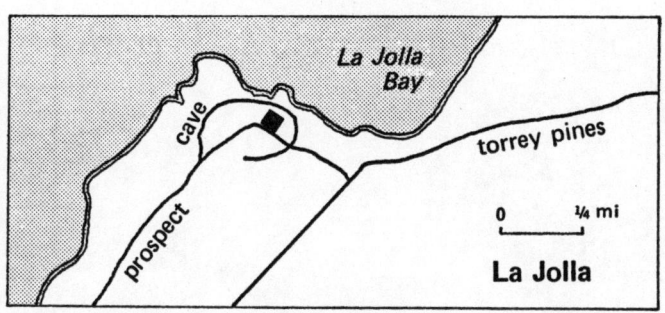

Schnitzelbank

This restaurant has been here for years. The interior has been done in a folksy German decor. The waitress wears the traditional dirndl. A friendly German spirit pervades the room.

Yet, it is not as popular as it could be—maybe because there is almost too much to eat. Most customers have difficulty finishing the meat, let alone all that accompanies it. And, while the food is good, it is not of the variety that compels one to rush back soon afterward for a little more of the same. This might be because there are few freshly cooked items available.

There is a wide choice of dinner possibilities. The wurst plates include two large potato pancakes, unfortunately not fried to order.

Hungarian goulash, as served here, is a meat stew flavored with spicy green pepper and served over soft noodles.

The meat loaf is primarily a liver loaf that has a refried look, as if prepared well in advance and then grilled to warm it when ordered. It is served with a delicious gravy and an egg.

Sauerbraten is also offered, as are other traditional German meats.

Warm potato salad and dry dark bread precede each entree A handsome dessert plate is brought on request, if you can look at more food after completing your meal.

Reservations are not necessary. Casual dress.

1037 Prospect St., La Jolla. (714) 454-4671
Daily: 11:30 - 9 (brunch served on Sun. 10:30 - 1)

Little Restaurants of San Diego / 45

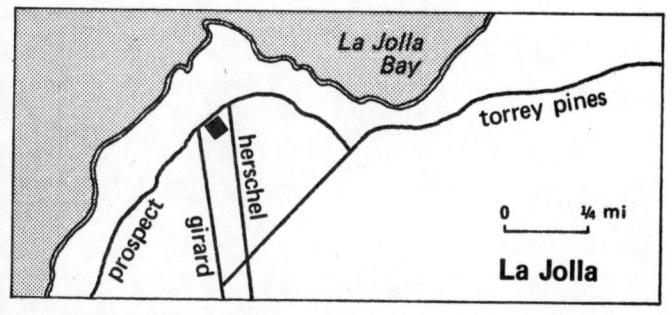

The Gatekeeper

The Gatekeeper is not a vegetarian restaurant nor is it strictly a health-foods restaurant. Rather, the liberal use of vegetables distinguishes its cuisine.

The organic tostada is popular because it is inexpensive and laden with vegetables, sprouts, and mushrooms. Steamed vegetables is a concoction of fresh broccoli, cauliflower, turnips, celery, carrots, and squash.

One cannot help but feel healthier after a heavy dose of all these fresh or steamed vitamins. However, with such abundance and generosity the individual flavors are apt to mingle promiscuously or fight with one another, as close relatives sometimes do.

In most respects the restaurant is a delight. It has been tastefully decorated; its intimate dining rooms have a lovely view of the water below and there is even a balcony for warm evenings. The proprietors seem concerned with the freshness of all the ingredients. The dinners are not expensive, starting under $4.

The Gatekeeper is a very popular place where a few minutes' wait is to be expected on any evening. Dress is varied and comfortable, from jeans to suits.

1294 Prospect St., La Jolla. (714) 459-0889
Weekdays 11:30 - 10; Sat. & Sun. 9 a.m. - 10 p.m.
No credit cards

Little Restaurants of San Diego / 47

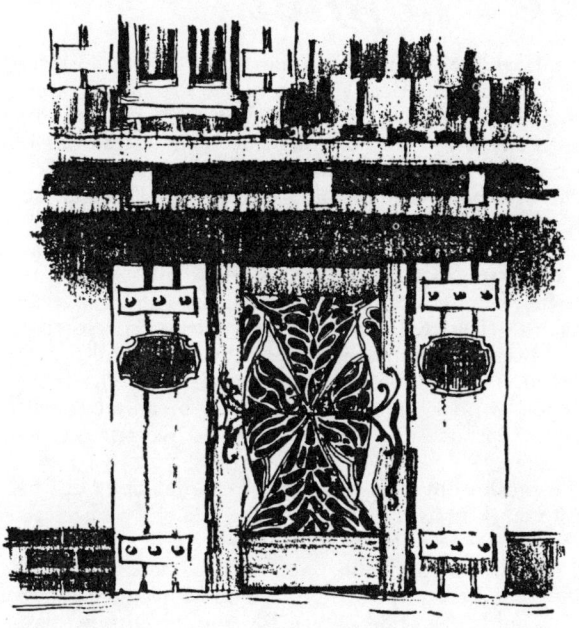

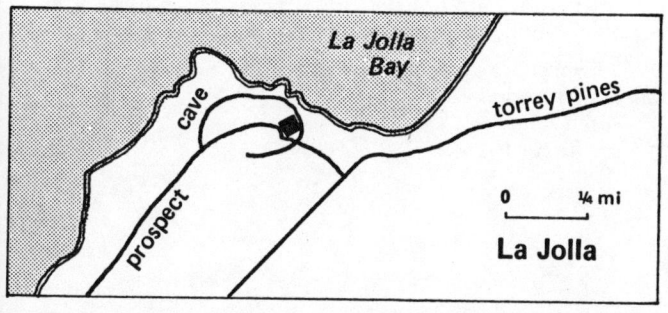

The Prophet

The least-likely place for a hard-core vegetarian restaurant is the Fairmont district. Yet, there the Prophet is, apparently thriving. It occupies two units in a stucco office building. Inside is another world. To one side is the restaurant filled with tables and plants. To the other side is a spacious carpeted waiting area with cushions and books. A little black box hidden behind some books produces quiet electronic bird calls. These have a calming effect—at least they did on me once I had solved the problem of where all the birds were.

Besides a long list of fruit drinks, teas, and appetizers, the menu offers two approaches to dinner. First there are the sandwiches. From a half-dozen or so possibilities, we tried two. The zucchini fritata was excellent. The fritata is put into the pocket of Bible (or Arab) bread along with tomatoes, sprouts, and other vegetables, flavorings, and seasonings.

The mushroom cheeseburger looked delicious but failed to taste as good as it looked, having a slightly bitter flavor.

The entrees vary from day to day. On one night we tried macaroni and cheese, egg foo yung, and a broccoli souffle. The best way to order would be to ask the waitress which would be a good choice for you, given your likes and dislikes in vegetables and seasonings. Each entree comes with tea, soup, salad, and a cooked vegetable (about $3).

This is a delightful and inexpensive way to dine. Friendliness and enthusiasm prevail throughout.

Reservations are not necessary. Dress tends to be comfortable. No alcohol, coffee, or smoking.

4461 University Ave., San Diego. (714) 283-7448
Tues. - Fri. noon - 2:30, 6 - 10; Sat. & Sun. 6 - 10;
   closed Mon.
No credit cards

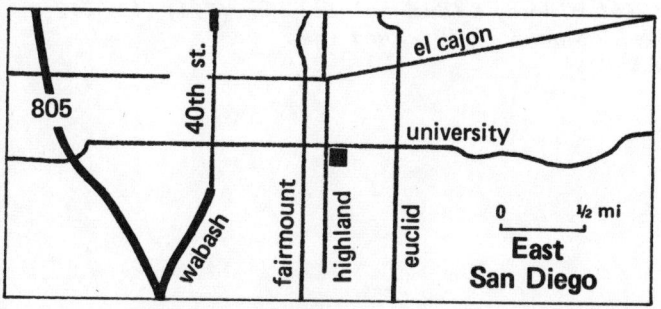

De Angelis

This is a fine Italian restaurant just east of El Cajon. Outside, peacocks cry on a nearby hill. Inside, on special occasions, Mr. De Angelis sings in a rich baritone voice. He is getting on in years, but for those few minutes he can transform a room of diners into members of a large warm family celebrating a special anniversary or birthday.

The menu is extensive, offering many pastas, veal dishes, seafood, and even steaks. The shrimp chef's special, for example, is a bit expensive but surprisingly good. The shrimp are large and whole, cooked in a light wine sauce that brings out some subtle flavors I had not tasted in shrimp before.

The chicken cannelloni are delicious as well. The pasta is homemade, with a rich, creamy texture and flavor. Into it is rolled a chicken mixture, and over it all goes tomato sauce.

The cheese ravioli are a little bland at first bite, but their delicate flavor begins to work on the tongue until you begin to wish that there were still more to be eaten. These are made from the same pasta recipe as the cannelloni. Over them is a smooth red sauce that proves to be completely unobtrusive.

All dinners include the usual minestrone, salad, and rolls—none of which we found at all remarkable, unfortunatel

Reservations should be made, especially on weekends. More dressy than casual.

12861 Highway 8 (Business), El Cajon. (714) 447-0842
Wed. - Mon. 5 - 9:30; closed Tues.
BA, MC

Little Restaurants of San Diego / 51

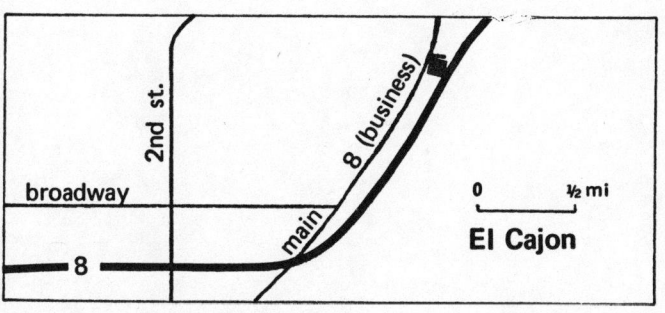

Giulio's

Ten years ago Giulio's had the reputation of serving the only authentic Italian food in San Diego. Today, despite some exterior remodeling, it may still claim that honor. Just ask the waiter about the food. He becomes positively eloquent when describing it.

There is a special dinner for two, offering a choice of spaghetti, ravioli, or lasagne and salad, bread, and wine, which has been selling for $7. However, there are better things on the menu which will not cost that much more.

The veal, for example, is excellent and quite filling. The veal saltimbocca, (breaded veal with prosciutto and cheese) has a wonderfully full flavor slightly on the salty side.

The scampi Giulio (shrimp cooked in garlic and wine) is spectacular. Both it and the veal are available as dinners that include soup or salad, spaghetti, and garlic bread.

Pastas, such as cannelloni, must be ordered *a la carte.* When in season, the melon with prosciutto provides a refreshing prelude to a dinner of pasta, whether ordered as a salad or appetizer.

The service is good; the dress is casual for some, dressy for others. Guilio's is a very comfortable place to eat excellent food. Reservations are advisable, though not necessary during the week.

809 Thomas St., San Diego. (714) 488-9126
Mon. - Sat. 5 - 11; Sun. 4 - 11
MC

Giulio's

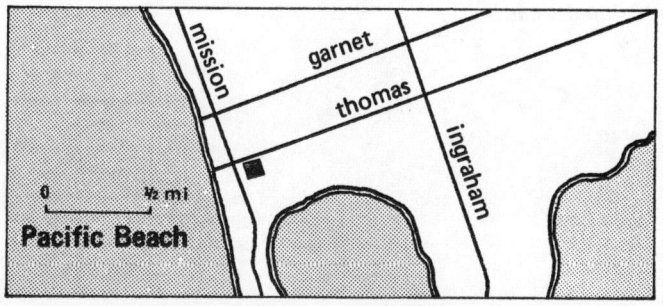

Nicolosi's

Although many people order from the pasta menu, for me Nicolosi's has always meant sandwiches and pizza. The restaurant is expanding to other locations (consult the phone book for addresses), but the mother site at 40th and El Cajon Blvd. still seems the best.

Nicolosi's is the favorite of those people who believe that pizza should have a thin crust. A thicker crust can be ordered, however, for $.50 extra. A good, spicy sauce is the essential ingredient. Pizza with pepperoni is about $2.50; combinations are more expensive.

The torpedo sandwich has always appealed to me. It is made in a long, narrow Italian bread roll with sliced meat. The meat forms a pocket into which go shredded lettuce and tomatoes. The special vinegar and oil dressing is then poured over the filling. It may be a little messy, but licking one's fingers is part of the enjoyment.

Both the meatball and sausage sandwiches are particularly good. The long torpedo roll is lined with meat, over which tomato sauce is ladled. You may find that a half-sandwich is more than enough for any light lunch or snack.

This is a restaurant, but any of the above items can be ordered to go. If you are eating there, the dress is very casual. Both light and dark beer are on tap.

4009 El Cajon Blvd., San Diego. (714) 282-9919
Mon. - Thurs. 11 - midnight; Fri. & Sat. 11 a.m. - 2 a.m.;
  Sun. noon - 10
No credit cards

Little Restaurants of San Diego / 55

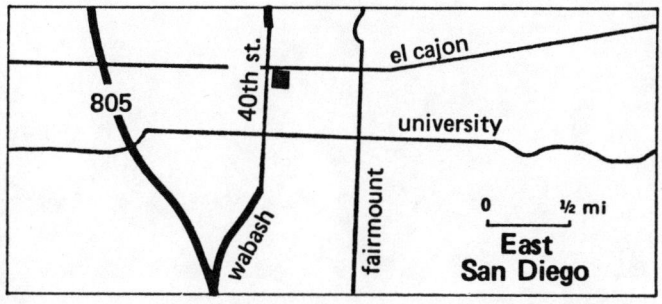

Venice

I do not recall eating anything other than pizza at Venice. It used to be my favorite years back, when the place had an older, less stylish decor and was as yet without that uninviting sign outside.

Now you are informed before you enter that there is a minimum order required and that bare feet will not be tolerated. If you can get past that sign and in the door, the worst is over and the best about to begin.

Pizzas come in one size, large enough for two normal people. The crust is moderately thick, soft with a hint of yeast. At first glance it may not look as though there is very much meat, for it is hidden under a sea of good cheese.

The pizza with sausage has been my consistent favorite. The management claims that it is homemade, which its special flavor does nothing to belie. As it cooks in the cheese, the sausage dissolves through the sauce, giving the entire pizza a rich, buttery flavor.

The dress is casual, of course: anything or nothing. Just don't forget those shoes.

3315 El Cajon Blvd., San Diego (714) 282-5200
Sun. - Thurs. noon - midnight; Fri. & Sat. noon - 2 a.m.
No credit cards

HOME STYLE
FOOD TO GO

adams
el cajon
university
40th st.
805
0
½ mi
East San Diego

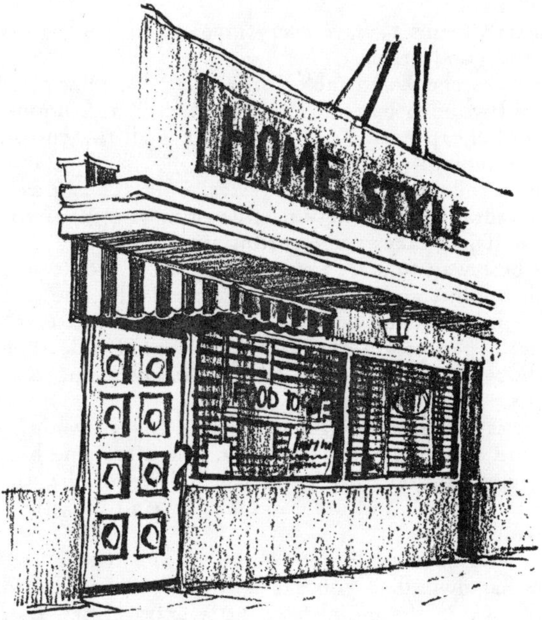

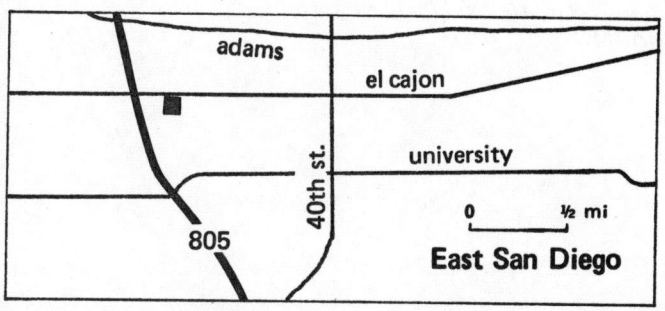

Zolezzi's

Zolezzi's seems to have everything: good food, good looks, and good prices.

There are checkered tablecloths, travel posters, plastic vines, and wooden barrels. There is wine at near-liquor-store prices and cheap beer. And the place has all the customers it can conveniently handle.

What is missing are the waitresses. Zolezzi's is a cafeteria-style restaurant, which may be fine once you get used to the idea—it just takes some getting used to.

The best way to start your evening there would be to go through the line and order a drink and maybe one of the delicious hot zucchini or artichoke fritatas to share as an appetizer. Then pick a nice table and relax awhile. The menu is on the wall to study when you are ready to make some decisions.

There is abalone stew for those cold foggy evenings when both hand and heart need warming. There are fine homemade ravioli covered with good sauce. There is the usual spaghetti and veal, and even a cod dish. And there is yet more wine.

Once you have made your decisions and the line at the counter has dwindled, you can leisurely place your order.

If you are in the mood for a little extra effort, Zolezzi's will reward you handsomely with good food at bargain prices. You can dress very casually, as well.

530 University Ave., San Diego. (714) 296-0975
Mon. - Sat. 10 - 8; closed Sun.
BA, MC

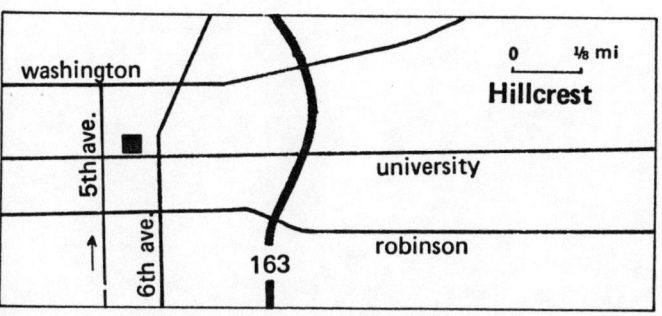

The Old Spaghetti Factory

The Factory is hardly a little restaurant, but who cares? Everything about it is perfect. It is gaily decorated with antiques and always full and happy. One is as apt to end up eating in a trolley car (in the middle of the immense dining room) or in a booth made out of a brass bed or heavy old doors as at a conventional round oak table. With that much variety, no two visits are alike.

The spaghetti is delicious and the prices rock-bottom. Of the six different sauces, each has its partisans. Our favorite is the spaghetti with browned butter and Mizithra cheese, a la Homer. Because the sauce is simply butter and cheese, it offers a pleasant change from the standard meat-sauce spaghetti of other restaurants or home-cooking fame.

Despite its location in a low-rent section of downtown, the restaurant is no secret. Reservations are not accepted, so a wait is unavoidable. If the wait is greater than your power to endure, drive up Fifth Ave. to Hillcrest and try Figaro's. It is a tiny restaurant with a large Italian menu, from pastas to spinach fritatas and veal, and moderate prices (741 W. Washington, 296-4811).

Fifth and K Sts., San Diego. (714) 233-4323
Sun. 4 - 10; Mon. - Thurs. 5 - 10; Fri. & Sat. 5 - midnight

Little Restaurants of San Diego / 61

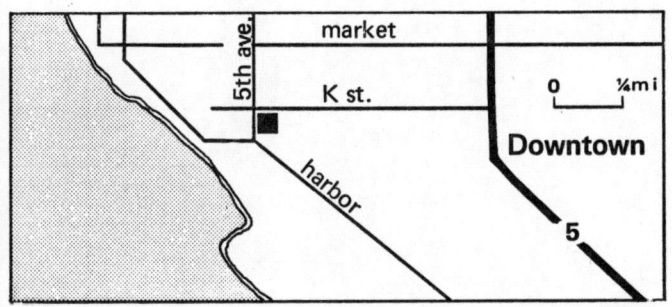

Miki-San

For a truly fine Japanese meal, one would hope for beautiful surroundings, graceful service, and delicately flavored food. Although missing some of these finer points, the Americanized Miki-San still offers reasonable Japanese food which we would recommend.

The food is mostly good and not without some interesting flavors, but it does seem to lack the loving attention and fresh seasonal vegetables that could make it really outstanding.

The tempura is worth trying if you are unfamiliar with that dish (batter-fried shrimp and vegetables). The sukiyaki is also good enough to try. The mizutake seemed to lack fresh vegetables and love, however.

Our meal was served as any corner cafe waitress would serve it. We missed the abundance of graceful service normally found at most authentic Japanese restaurants.

The surroundings at Miki-San are merely ordinary, but a recent decision by city officials allowing cooking at restaurant tables could change the food, service, and atmosphere immensely.

All the dinners are served with soup, rice, and tea. Families are not an uncommon sight. Most patrons seemed dressed in their good casual clothes. Reservations are advisable.

2424 5th Ave., San Diego. (714) 235-4330
Tues. - Sun. 11:30 - 10; Fri. & Sat. 11:30 - 11;
  closed Mon.
BA, MC

Little Restaurants of San Diego / 63

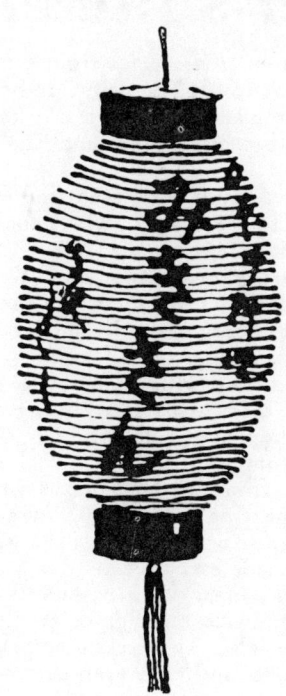

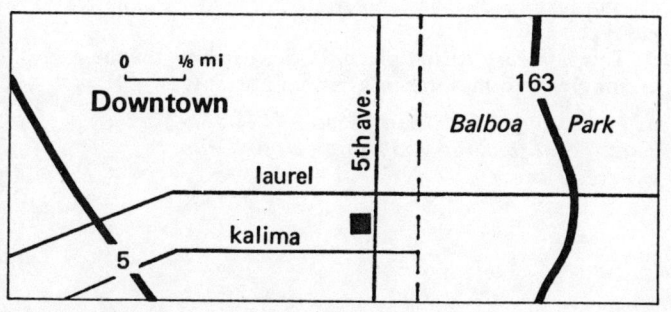

Blumer's Bakery

Blumer's is a no-nonsense place from entrance to exit. The booths are functional. The lights are bright enough so there can be no mistaking what is on the menu or plate. The waitresses are brusque and abrupt. The service is fast. Pay the cashier.

A romantic hideaway it is not. But the food is good—and almost exotic for San Diego, where such delicatessen-restaurants are rarities.

For a few dollars one can order a full dinner, such as brisket of beef with potatoes, soup, and the like. However, it will probably be more enjoyable and rewarding to try some of the stranger things on the menu.

There is chicken soup with matzo balls. While this kind of chicken soup is thought by many to have amazing curative powers, the matzo balls are there simply to taste good and fill the tummy.

Tomato herring from Scotland makes a fine light dinner on a hot day. A meat or potato knish sounds great, but Blumer's never seems to have them. (The waitress assured me that they are made every Wednesday.)

Lox (sliced raw salmon) on a bagel with cream cheese makes a terrific sandwich morning or evening. Cheese blintzes are a treat, also. They resemble pancakes folded around cream cheese, and taste even better than they sound.

After you have thoroughly annoyed the waitress by asking to try all of these, and if you are still hungry, there are familiar sandwiches and some unfamiliar omelettes to enjoy.

This is a very casual place. It can get busy in the early evening, which may mean a few minutes' wait.

5379 El Cajon Blvd., San Diego. (714) 582-2791
Tues. - Sun. 8 a.m. - 8:30 p.m.; closed Mon.
No credit cards

COFFEE
SHOP
Blumers
BAKERY

0 ¼ mi
East
San Diego
el cajon
university
fairmount
euclid
54th st.

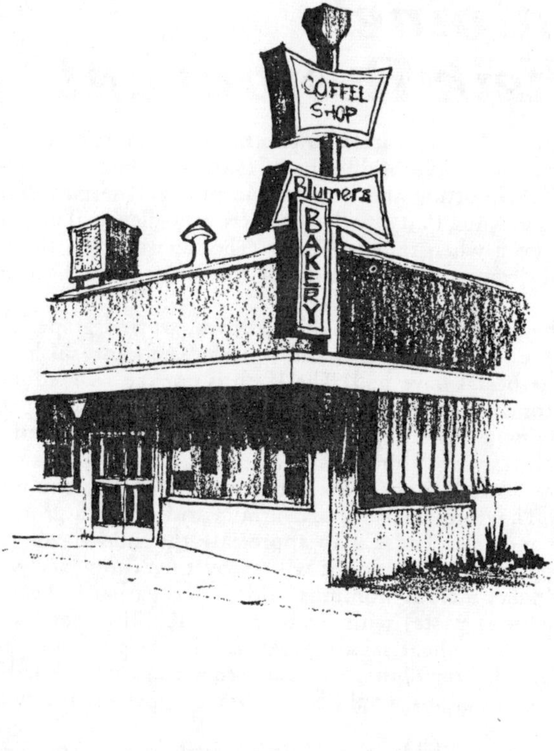

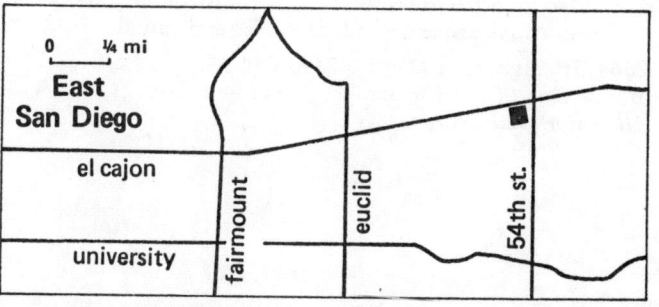

Antoine's Sheik Restaurant

Antoine's works hard to capture the atmosphere we associate with the Middle East—that of curtained rooms for silent plotting and hushed conspiracy. The two dining rooms are not that small, but there is a silence that pervades them even when they are busy. The tapestries on the walls and the water pipes on most of the tables contribute to the aura.

The menu consists of shish kebabs, stuffed grape leaves, cabbage leaves, eggplant, and squash. The lamb shish kebabs are the best I have had. The lamb is cooked to medium-rare. The tomato is soft and warm, making a superb companion to the meat. The pepper and onion are not as attractive, though they are almost as good.

The stuffed grape leaves are not as exotic as one might wish. They are small tubular affairs stuffed with ground meat and rice. Those who appreciate the mild flavor of the grape leaves no doubt will enjoy them immensely.

Dinners include hommus (a delicious garbanzo-bean/sesame-seed paste) with Arab bread, tabouli (a parsley and cracked-wheat salad), green salad, rice pilaf, and bread.

For a lighter dinner one can order *a la carte*. A half-order of hommus would be an ample appetizer for two people.

Wine is available, though it is a little more expensive than in some other restaurants. Cocktails can also be ordered.

Reservations are accepted. Dress is semi-casual.

2664 5th Ave., San Diego. (714) 234-5888
Mon. - Fri. 11 - 9:30; Sat. 4 - 10; closed Sun.
All major credit cards

Little Restaurants of San Diego / 67

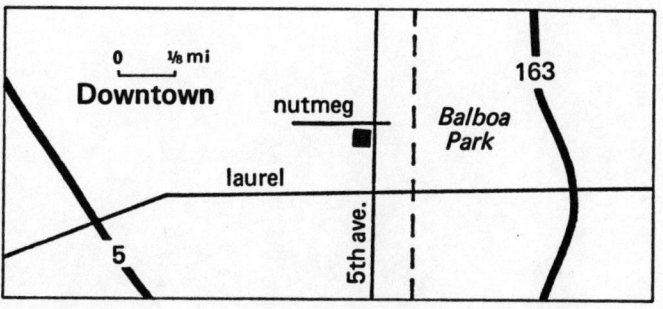

Alfonso's Hideway

Good food makes people happy. And good Mexican food is enough to make any person lightheaded and gay, from anticipation to satiation. This partly explains the festive atmosphere at Alfonso's. The food is the best and the portions are never stingy.

Try the carne asada taco, a wonderful example of imaginative and flavorful cooking. Chunks of char-broiled steak with onions and sauces make the filling. Two soft-fried corn tortillas hold the hot meat.

Another delight is the quesadilla suprema—a rich mixture of shredded beef and cheese folded in a huge flour tortilla. The cheese enchilada is also excellent. There are a few surprises on the menu, such as the flautas and sopes.

Alfonso's is the restaurant end of a bar called the Court Room (which, no doubt, assists in creating the festive atmosphere.) But do not let this deter you. At night it is all restaurant and good food.

Despite the high quality of the food and the chic location, this is a very inexpensive Mexican restaurant. Dress is casual. Reservations necessary only for parties of six or more.

1015 Prospect St., La Jolla. (714) 454-7655
Sun. 11:30 - 9:30; Mon. - Thurs. 11:30 - 10; Fri. & Sat. 11:30 - midnight
BA, MC

Little Restaurants of San Diego / 69

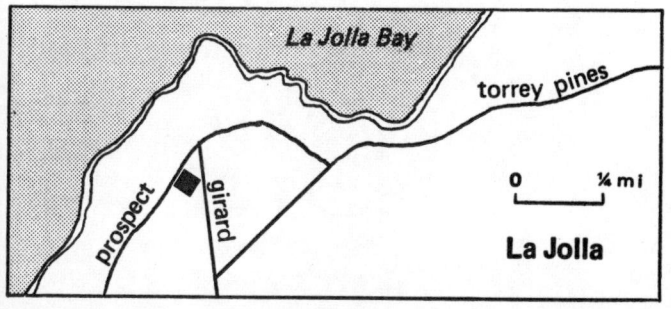

Aljones

The name of this restaurant comes not from a particularly apt Mexican word but from the owner, Mr. Jones—Al, to his friends. He and his wife, who acts as the hostess, converted an old house into the restaurant, using the living rooms for dining areas and transforming a porch into an outdoor eating area.

Our favorite from the menu has always been the chicken burrito with sour cream. It is a flour tortilla stuffed with plenty of chicken and then lightly covered with sauce and lots of melted sour cream.

Another dish they do well is chile relleno. The batter over the chile is especially thick and fluffy. The cheese within is American, rather than the white cheese many prefer. Over it is a fine sauce filled with onions, tomatoes, and peppers.

The dinners are attractively served in this friendly family restaurant. Dress is casual, and reservations are not necessary. Cocktails, wine, and beer—domestic and imported—are available.

860 Garnet Ave., San Diego. (714) 488-6282
Daily: 5 - 10
BA, MC

Little Restaurants of San Diego / 71

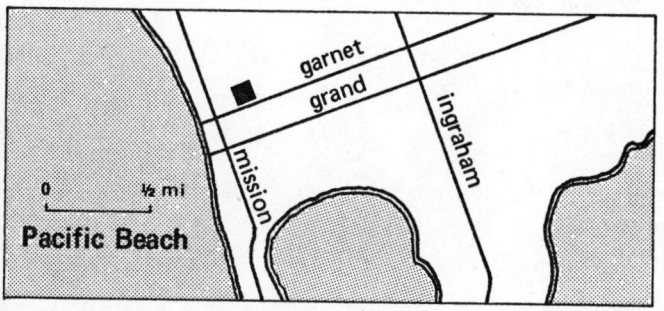

Bea's Rancho Chico

After midnight the pace slows a bit at Bea's. The loud talking and laughing of the early evening are subdued. People linger at their tables, now. There is no hurry. The food has been leisurely eaten and they can lean back to share a conversation as they have shared a meal.

This is a much more pleasant place to go after-hours on a weekend than is the local hamburger stand. And, unless you know an exceptional hamburger stand, the food is much better.

There is a good taco, for example, filled with freshly shredded lettuce. The enchilada is loaded with plenty of melted cheese and covered with a decent sauce. The burrito has a tomato-soup-style sauce that is a little too sweet.

It is nice in Bea's early or late. The arrangement of the tables gives the restaurant an intimate, homey feeling. The plain decor and the quietly efficient service contribute to that some feeling.

The Rancho Chico is a popular place, but there seems always to be a table ready for you. The dress is very casual and comfortable.

4857 El Cajon Blvd., San Diego. (714) 583-3005
Tues. - Thurs. 11 a.m. - midnight; Fri. & Sat. 11 a.m. - 3 a.n
  Sun. noon - 10; closed Mon.
No credit cards

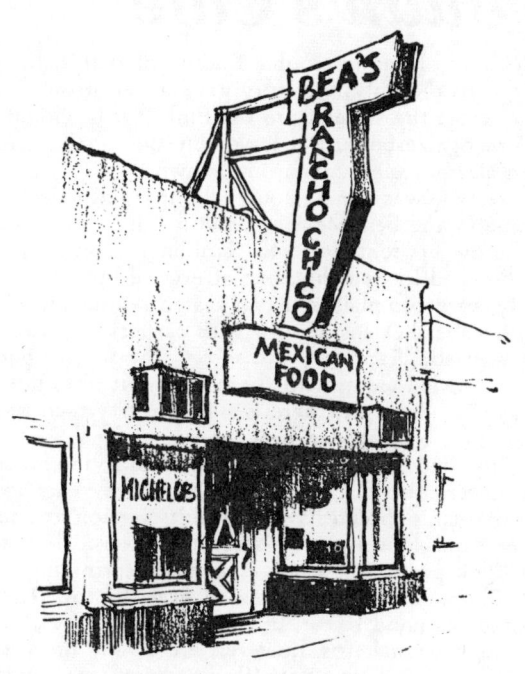
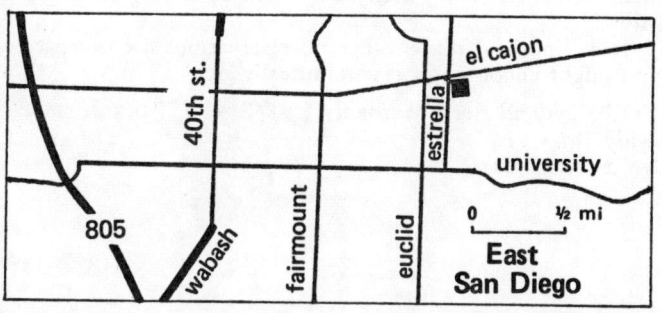

El Juan's Café

You should have no trouble finding El Juan's, for it is next door to the only two-story gas station in the city and directly across the street from the Pink Pig. It should be easy to recognize because it looks like one of the many restored classic restaurants around town.

For years it was a marvelously dumpy place that sold some of the best Mexican food north of the border. Then the owners remodeled the building. As in most such cases, the food looked the same afterward but there probably were complaints that it tasted remodeled as well.

El Juan's is slick inside now with carpets, a glitter ceiling, a plastic grapevine, and so on. The food is good; if it was remodeled along with the building, it does not taste that way. For example, there is a fine hearty taco full of large portions of shredded beef.

We also tried the specialty, a "Mexican flying saucer." Flying saucers quit fascinating the Air Force years ago, and maybe El Juan's should have retired its version at about the same time. It is a giant tostada based on a flour tortilla. Over a thick portion of beans is a liberal sprinkling of hamburger. Chopped lettuce is spooned over the top. The result is a tostada of good flavor, but far too dry to be great.

The huevos rancheros, however, are among the best available. The sauce is coarse with chopped tomatoes, onions, and peppers. It is poured over two eggs cooked so that the whites are firm and the yolks runny. Refried beans are not included—a deficiency easily corrected by asking for a side order.

It is a popular place. Since no reservations are accepted, you might encounter a few minutes' wait.

2316 Highland Ave., National City. (714) 477-6262
Daily: 11 - 11
No credit cards

Little Restaurants of San Diego / 75

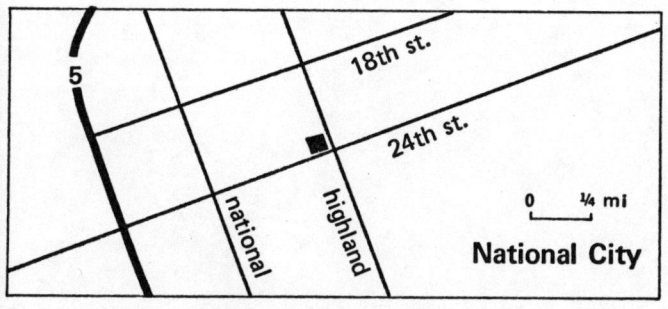

Rosendo's Hideway

If Rosendo's is paying thousands annually in bribes in order to maintain its hideaway status, I would suggest that the attempt is not working. Too many people are there eating dinner—especially during the racing season—to indicate that any such bribes have helped steer people in the wrong direction.

Rosendo's is a nice country Mexican restaurant. The food is good, competently prepared. Prices are about average—some more, some less.

It is a big place, dark enough inside to hide away a posse. Parties of four or six, common the night we were there, can remain lost for hours. Here and there around the walls are placed some interesting antique pieces. However, in order to see any of these at night, you will have to rely on occasional flashes of lightning.

Reservations are not required. Dress is a sort of neat casual.

Carmel Valley Road (east), Del Mar. (714) 755-3223
Tues. - Fri. 11:30 - 2, 5 - 10; Sat. & Sun. 5 - 10;
  closed Mon.
MC

Little Restaurants of San Diego / 77

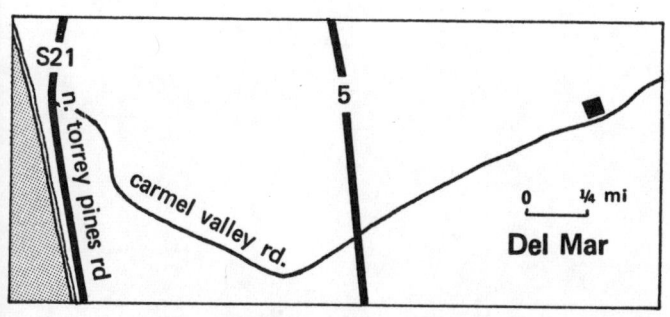

Polish

Three Mermaids

A pierogi is a Polish dumpling, a lot like a ravioli. Beer soup is reminiscent of thin, hot eggnog. A Polish sausage is a first-rate hot dog.

These are a few of the "Polish delights" at the Three Mermaids restaurant. As presented here, the national cuisine is not strange at all, but vaguely reminiscent of other dishes with new flavors. Like the crepe filled with sauerkraut—it is startling, but likable.

The restaurant used to boast that it served "no junk food," which is mostly true now. Ingredients are freshly prepared, though some packaged mixes can be detected. Polish servings are generous and filling.

The decor is plain, without elaborate adornments. Dinners are about $3, which makes Polish prices the best around. Dress is casual. This is a good place to come with a party of four or more: groups have more fun and each person gets to taste the others' food. Reservations not necessary. No alcoholic beverages served.

3539 Adams Ave., San Diego. (714) 281-3729
Mon. - Fri. noon - 2, 5 - 9; Sat. & Sun. 5 - 9; closed Tues.
No credit cards

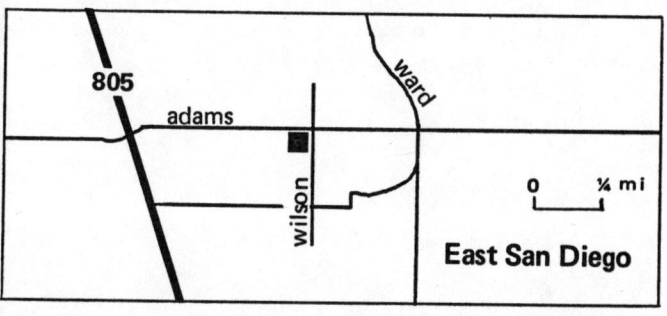

80 / Seafood/American/Chinese

Tom Lai's

This should be a terrible restaurant. In the first place, it is not a little restaurant at all. It is a very large place filled with people and bustling waiters. Then, too, it has windows opening on the bay, which often means that the view outsparkles the mediocre fare. Finally, it has a giant menu offering three different cuisines. And when a place tries to please all comers, it generally succeeds in pleasing none.

However, Mr. Lai makes this restaurant work. He cares about the quality of food served and worries about the price. As a result, you can get pork chops, lamb chops, liver, prime rib, or a Sunday duck or turkey for only a few dollars. Or you can order seafood such as abalone, sea bass, rock cod, halibut, or oysters for $3 or less (and in most cases it will be less).

The dinners come complete with appetizer, soup, salad, rolls, baked potato, coffee, and dessert. All the food is well prepared and home-cooked, including the four pies offered as dessert. This side of Tom Lai's menu is so good, we have not the courage to try the Chinese side for fear of disappointment.

Without reservations, you will have to suffer a wait in the bar watching the lights play across the waters. With or without reservations, request a window table: it will be worth the extra minutes' wait. Dress casually and bring the family. At these prices you can afford to treat them.

For a reliable, inexpensive meal with a view and cocktails, Tom Lai's has no equal.

1355 W. G St., San Diego. (714) 234-1584
Tues. - Sat. 11:30 - 10; Sun. noon - 9; closed Mon.
No credit cards

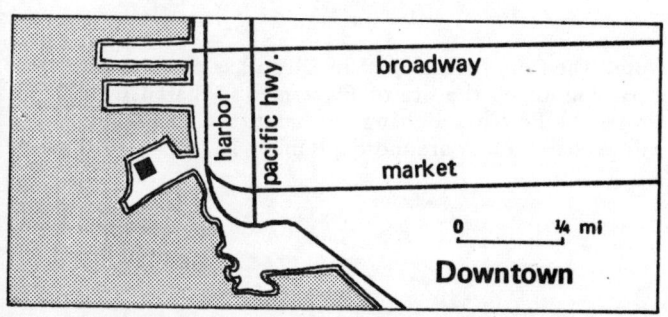

Fishermen's Wharf Grotto

Some of what people say about the Grotto is true. It does command a nice view of the sport-fishing wharf. At night the boats are being readied for their next day out on the high sea. Their lights are on and their owners are busy hauling aboard fishing gear, beer, and Dramamine.

It is also true that the Grotto is an unpretentious sort of place, that it serves seafood, and that its prices are reasonable.

When people start to say that the food is great, a bit of skepticism is required. It does have a great sourdough bread. I found it irresistible. It also serves some decent entrees, such as totuava and swordfish.

The rest of the dinners are not so reliable. Given a choice of soup or salad, choose the salad. The Manhattan clam chowder proved to be a tepid clam-flavored vegetable soup.

There is also a choice between potatoes au gratin and french-fried potatoes. Opt for the french fries.

The view from either floor is worth insisting on a window table. This should be done when making reservations, because neither bar is a comfortable waiting room. Dress seems to be semi-casual.

2945 Garrison St., San Diego. (714) 222-3137
Daily: 11 - 11
All major credit cards

Note: The Port District of San Diego has plans to put a parking lot on the site of Fishermen's Wharf Grotto. Unless the Port has a change of heart, the restaurant will probably close around September 15, 1974.

CAFE

nimitz
n. harbor dr.
garrison
0
½ mi
Point Loma
rosecrans
scott

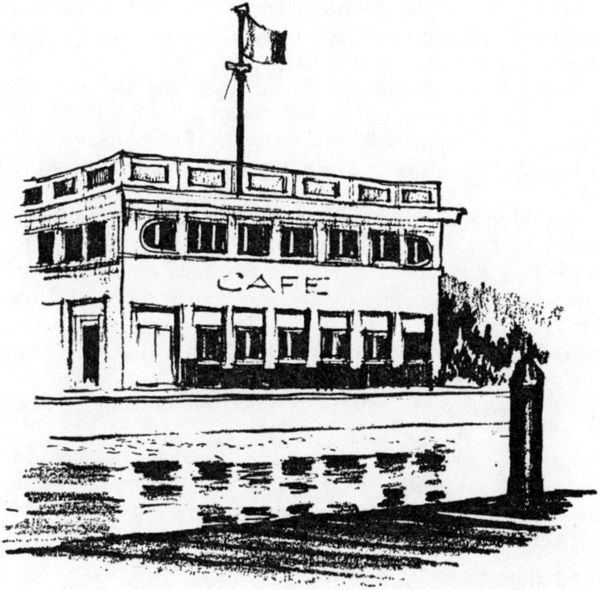

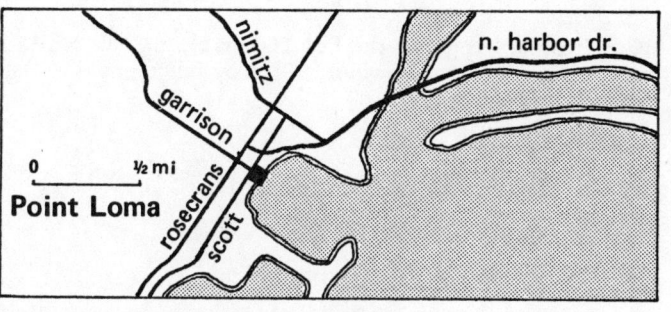

The Fish Place

Of all the new restaurants around town which are lavish and imaginative in their use of wood, The Fish Place is the tiniest and one of the best. It is long and narrow, with high-backed sculpted-wood booths on each side and a row of smaller booths in a serpentine design up the middle. The booths are comfortable and intimate. For parties larger than four, a call in advance to ensure accommodations would be wise.

For lunch or a light dinner, a fine abalone sandwich is available. The meat is lightly breaded and cooked just long enough to preserve its flavor. It is served on large slices of a rich white bread, lightly toasted, and includes lettuce and sliced tomatoes. The sandwich comes with a dinner salad (served in an abalone shell) or rice pilaf (about $2.50).

Each of the dinners—totuava, fish of the day (price varies), mahi-mahi, shrimp teriyaki, and shrimp—is preceded by a dinner salad and served with rice pilaf and bread. Fresh green onions are sliced into the rice. The bread is particularly appealing in that it has a strip of raisins through the middle of each slice, enriching the good brown taste.

Dress is casual.

3784 Ingraham St., San Diego. (714) 274-0172
Mon. - Thurs. 11:30 - 2, 5 - 10; Fri. & Sat. 5 - 11;
  Sun. 5 - 10
No credit cards

Note: Rumor has it that the Fish Place is closing this location and moving elsewhere. Check by telephone before you go.

Little Restaurants of San Diego / 85

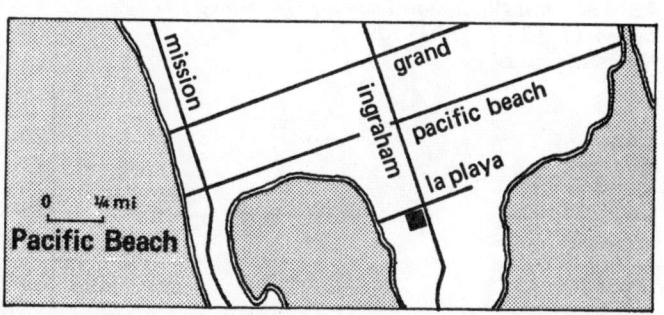

Krishna Mulvaney

The interior is the best part of this or any Krishna's. It is a gallimaufry of ingenious decorations, textures, panels, louvers, and windows.

The seafood and vegetable half of the menu is moderately priced but not as spectacular tasting as one expects in these surroundings. Accompanying all dinners is the familiar salad bar replete with soup and bread. From all the offerings our favorite was the mud pie made from coffee ice cream, a touch of chocolate syrup and whipped cream. It would make a fine late night treat.

It is an inordinately popular restaurant, so expect a wait. If you cannot abide waiting there is more room across the street at Krishna's Swan Song. This interior is even more striking than that of its parent. North African in appearance, the stark white walls and red tile floor are cooled by skylights and hanging ferns.

The cuisine is warm courses of beef, fowl, fish, and vegetables in the guise of skewers, crepes, and a few other miscellanies—like the fish stew, hearty enough for any cold winter's night.

We also enjoyed the beef and breast, a teriyaki combination of chicken breast and strips of flank steak. The tempura is not expensive and includes a generous dose of shrimp.

Dress is very casual, just pretend you're going or returning from the beach. No reservations are accepted.

4230 Mission Blvd., San Diego. (714) 488-5142
Daily: 11:30 - 2, 5:30 - 11
No credit cards

Little Restaurants of San Diego / 87

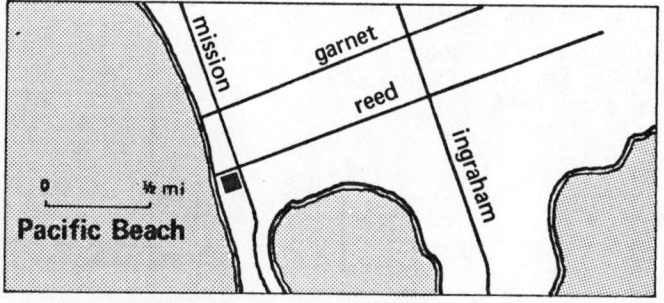

Ocean Fresh Seafood Café

In the old days the inevitable accouterments of every seafood restaurant were stuffed fish. Dusty old fish, in colors that never disgraced any living thing, hung from the walls. Each had been given a glassy eye that stared down on the tables below, frightening every child in the room into believing that what he was now eating was that very fish.

Stuffed fish are out of vogue, now, as are captains' chairs at round tables adorned with bowls of oyster crackers. But some of the traditional seafood decor has been preserved at Ocean Fresh, where a marlin still oversees part of the dining below and the plain wooden booths retain a bit of that old-salt flavor.

Prices at Ocean Fresh are like the good old days. So is the fish. It is fresh. (A fish market adjoins the dining room.) Portions are generous; service is friendly. Dinners include a salad and french fries made of old-fashioned real potatoes. Most dinners are under $3. Sandwiches, such as abalone, crab, and swordfish, are available for about $2.

The treat here is cracked crab. Taken from the case at the current price per pound, it is served at your table for only a $.75 preparation charge. Unfortunately, the wine list is not adequate, though bottles are reasonably priced.

Reservations are not necessary. Dress casually. (Ocean Fresh operates a sister restaurant in La Jolla.)

183 Broadway, Chula Vista. (714) 427-3050
Mon. - Sat. 11 - 10; Sun. 11 - 9
No credit cards

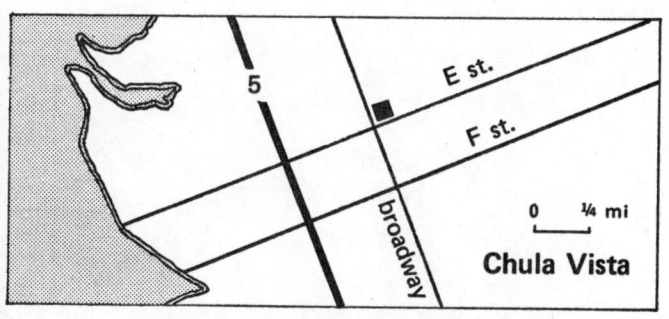

World Famous

Its location near the ocean on the boardwalk makes this a great place to dine. During daylight hours there is a fine view of the beach. At night, the atmosphere within is as warm and friendly as the service. The food is spectacular.

The menu is limited so that the staff can concentrate on the quality of the food. Sea bass, a combination plate, abalone and three steak combinations are listed.

Each dinner comes with salad—a large dinner plate of lettuce with a couple of cherry tomatoes and a generous portion of salad dressing—and a basket of warm whole-wheat bread.

For one entree, we chose abalone. To our surprise, there were three fillets, more than the plate could adequately handle. It appeared more like a stack of flapjacks than a plate of seafood. Special consideration is given to the breading, which is carefully seasoned. When the abalone is tender it does the old melting-in-the-mouth number.

The same evening the "catch of the night" was swordfish, which we found irresistible. It, too, filled the platter. It was about the size of a prime rib, only thicker, and had been charcoal-broiled to retain the flavor.

Fresh corn (in season) and potatoes are each only $.35. Cocktails are now available at reasonable prices.

No reservations are accepted, so you can expect crowds on weekends. The dress tends to be outrageous.

701 Thomas St., San Diego. (714) 488-1808
Daily: 11 - 2, 5:30 - 11
BA, MC

Little Restaurants of San Diego / 91

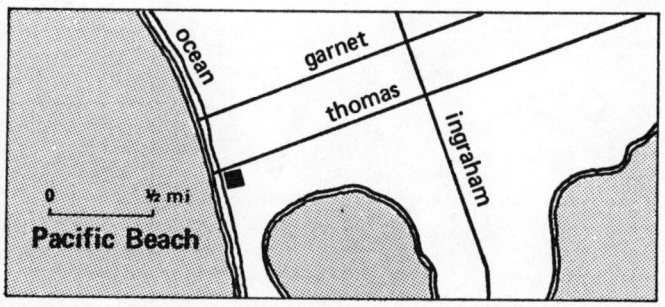

Nordic Inn

According to my Danish informant, the Nordic Inn has the best smorgasbord in town. All the others are poor imitations, he tells me. If its lunch and dinner business is any indication, he is not alone in his opinion. The parking lot is full and so are the many booths inside.

Neither the format nor the kind of food offered is unique. There are bean salads, green salads, jello salads, pickled herring, fruit, vegetables, etc., as well as two kinds of chicken, stuffed peppers, Swedish meatballs, roast beef, and fish. (Fewer meats are offered at lunchtime.) It all looked the same as in similar restaurants, but I will admit that the food tasted better than I remember having elsewhere.

The prices are reasonable enough. A call first will let you know what they are currently charging. Beverages are extra. No beer or wine.

No reservations. Come as you are, with shoes.

3577 Midway Dr., San Diego. (714) 233-7721
Daily: 11 - 4 (lunch), 4 - 8:30 (dinner)
BA

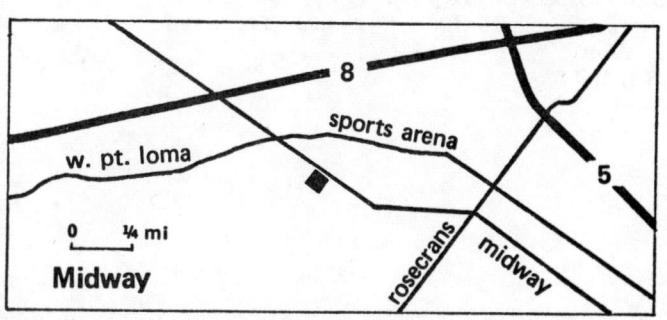

Restaurant Madrid

Spanish food should not be confused with the more familiar (to Californians) Mexican cuisine: More than an ocean separates the two. One is tortilla and beans while the other is wine and garlic, rice and seafood.

Paella, a combination of seafood and rice, is probably the most popular and famous Spanish dish. When prepared well, as it is here, saffron coats each kernel of rice and the clams, crab, scallops, shrimp, calamari, and chunks of chicken covering the bed of rice retain their individual flavors.

Mariscada, another popular entree, is not unlike a bouillabaisse: shellfish and red snapper combined in a wonderful tomato-wine-garlic sauce. Pollo al Avila, chicken in a cream-and-wine sauce, is full of garlic, fresh peas, and pimento—a welcome alternative to the standard deep-fried or baked version.

Other entrees here include stuffed trout, steak in wine, shrimp with garlic, and sole wrapped in paper. The portions are large and the ingredients seem as fresh as season and availability allow. On the *a la carte* menu, entrees average just over $5; soup, salad, and an appetizer would add $2 or so.

The decor is not sumptuous, but a recent remodeling should develop the possibilities in this interesting room. The sangria is fruity and refreshing, and even the American coffee deserves an *ole!*

916 Prospect St., La Jolla (714) 459-3734
Tues. - Fri. 5 - 10:30: Sat. - Sun. 5 - 11; closed
   Mon.
BA, MC

Little Restaurants of San Diego / 95

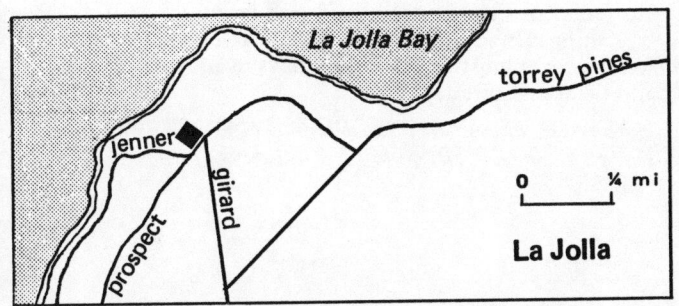

Anthony's Star of the Sea

If you happen to have a guest who needs impressing, Anthony's is a good place to begin. It offers elegant dining at a substantial price. There is a view of the harbor. There are chandeliers, upholstered chairs, and tables set in the grand manner. And the continental service can be smooth, if a bit impersonal. Of course, as in most restaurants of this class, you will be able to impress your guest all the more if you are known to the staff. The extra smiles and courtesies such familiarity breeds can be extremely impressive.

A good start to the meal would be the hors d'oeuvre tray, which offers bits and pieces of seafood delights. There are oysters Rockefeller, stuffed clams, steamed crab, asparagus wrapped in fresh salmon, cherry tomatoes stuffed with shrimp, and something I suspect is pickled abalone. (The order for two people is plenty for a party of four.)

One can order either Manhattan or New England-style clam chowder. Both are good and enjoyed by their respective fans. However, the latter lacks that fresh cream flavor I appreciate in chowder.

The entrees are too numerous to mention. Of our four dinners, the most spectacular was the seafood brochette, a kabob of fish and shellfish which is set on fire at the table. The best to eat was the abalone, which is a small abalone served whole. The most disappointing was a fish stuffed with shrimp and served in a heavy sauce.

During the summer season this is a very popular place. Reservations must be made four days in advance. A coat and tie are required.

Harbor Dr. at Ash St., San Diego. (714) 232-7408
Daily: 5:30 - 10:30; closed on holidays
BA, MC

Little Restaurants of San Diego / 97

Aspen Mine Co.

The Aspen Mine Co. can be recognized easily by the litter of barrels and rusting mine carts on the premises. Once you find a parking place, you can enter through a mine shaft that has little plants growing from niches in one wall.

In the depths of the Mine it is dimly lit. Only gradually does the eye begin to make out the huge timbers surrounding the booths in the dining area, the stained glass, and the curiosities attached to the walls.

Given the average waiting time for dinner, which can be an hour or more, you will have plenty of time to explore. A turn down one shaft will lead you to the Slope Room, where drinks flow and movies or slides are shown. Enough people think the food is worth waiting for to make this one of the area's most popular restaurants.

The prime rib is consistantly good. The crab, the other half of the shell and rib combination plate, is cooked tender and succulent. Also on the menu are steaks, trout, swordfish and a fondue.

Reservations are not accepted. The dress is a classy casual, for most people.

5880 El Cajon Blvd., San Diego. (714) 582-1813
Mon. & Tues. 11 - 2:30, 5 - 11; Wed. - Fri. 11 - 2:30,
5 - midnight; Sat. 5 - 12:45; Sun. 10 - 2 (brunch),
4 - 11
AE, BA, MC

Little Restaurants of San Diego / 99

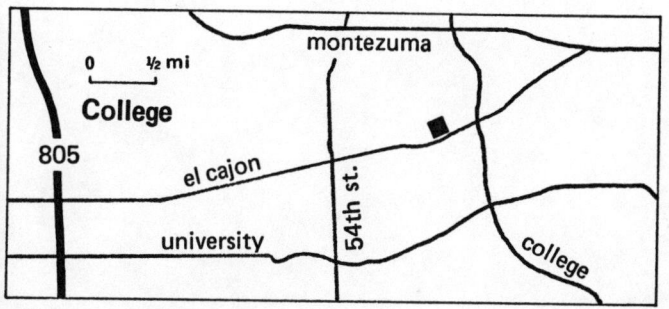

Chart House

Ask any female hitchhiker and she will tell you that the best restaurant around is the Chart House. It must be true because the place is filled with folk, hitchhikers and otherwise. It has a stylish, attractive interior with a fine view of the coastline and Torrey Pines. The service is friendly and observant, showing a real concern for the welfare of the patrons

This is a steak house, so it is wise to order steak, or maybe lobster if it is in season. Besides steak, prime rib, shrimp, and lobster, the menu lists an artichoke and ratatouille. The latter is especially for green-pepper lovers, being primarily peppers and a sprinkling of other vegetables in a stewed-tomato sauce with a thick coating of melted cheese over the top. Dinners include unlimited trips to the salad bar, baskets of bread, cups of coffee or tea, and dishes of ice cream. Potatoes are extra.

The wine list is small but varied. No reservations are taken, which means a long wait during the summer season and on weekends. A call to the restaurant should give an indication of how long it will be. A window table is worth a few extra minutes' wait. Dress is a well-tailored casual. Chart Houses also can be found on Coronado and Shelter Island.

1270 Prospect St., La Jolla. (714) 459-8201
Daily: 5:30 - 10:30
BA, MC

La Jolla Bay
torrey pines
cave
prospect
0
¼ mi
La Jolla

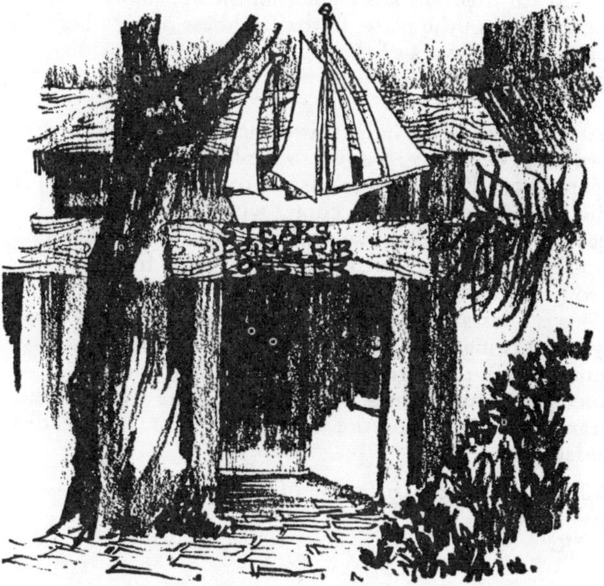

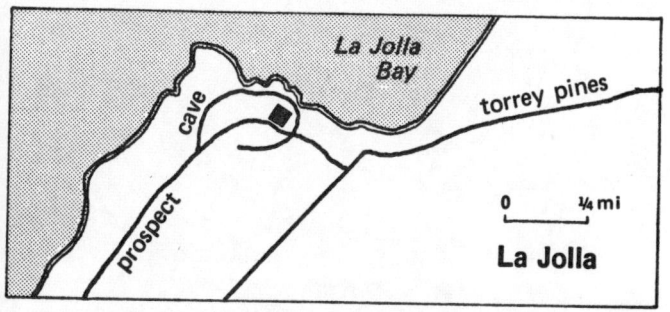

Chez Francois

Food is prepared with love at Chez Francois. The staff's fondness for their work is evident in the appealing arrangement of food on the plate, in the freshness of each ingredient, in the delicate flavors of the sauces, and in the obvious pride with which each course is first described and then served.

After you've eaten here, it is difficult to show any restraint in ordering. Certainly, for two, one plate of fine, freshly prepared hors d'oeuvre (such as the oysters Rockefeller) is sufficient. Since the dinner comes with salad and soup, one does not really need a bowl of the onion soup, however tempting it might be. But the desserts, made fresh daily, are so good that restraint is folly. Order at least one each.

This is a restaurant for those who will accept only the very best-tasting food. With such food, once the meal has begun it's easy to overlook the other pleasantries at Francois—the furnishings, the prints, and the vintage wines in transparent crypts on the walls. Reservations are recommended.

5662 La Jolla Blvd., La Jolla. (714) 459-6066
Daily: 6 - 11
BA, MC

Chez Francois
FRENCH
RESTAURANT

0
¼ mi
La Jolla
bird rock
la jolla
la jolla mesa
turquoise

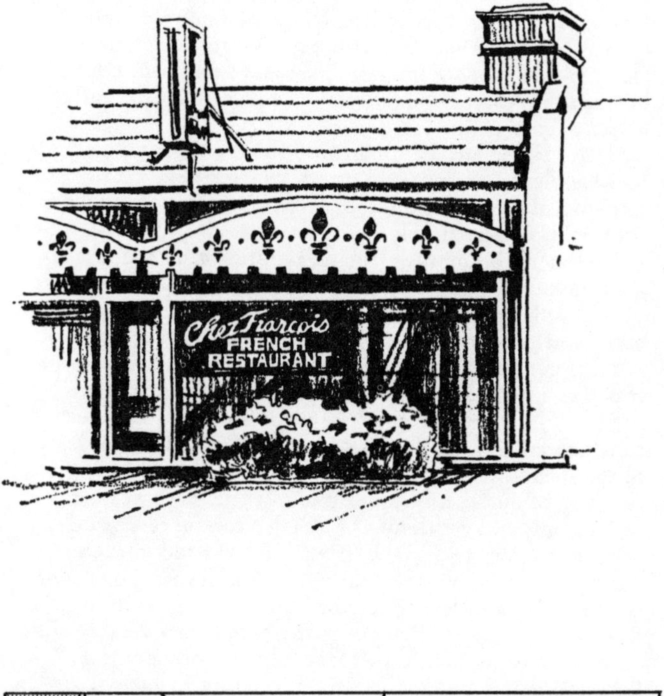

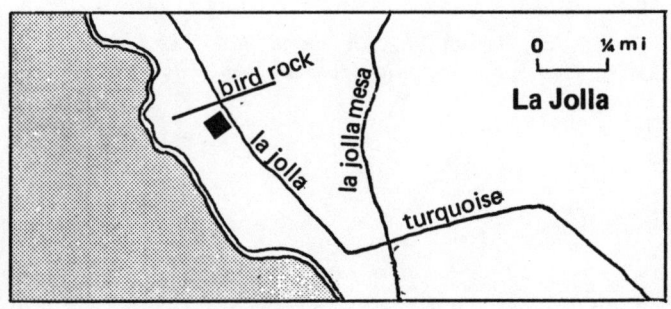

Lubach's

The venerable Lubach's is considered one of San Diego's finest restaurants. Yearly it wins the *Holiday* magazine award for excellence. Its name signifies to most San Diegans the ultimate in good taste and fine food. Because of this reputation it is for many the place for celebrating with a special meal.

There is one large dining room filled with rows of booths, plenty of light and a very chic din: clinking glasses, clanking silverware, trundling carts, bustling waiters, and conversation desperately rising above it all.

The menu befits the size and reputation of the restaurant, having both variety and depth. Everything is expensive here, so abandon all thought of pecuniary responsibility and order only the best. If you order wisely you should spend the evening enjoying one of the fine seafood appetizers or the escargot, the rich turtle soup, and an entree of lamb or a freshly caught and cooked fish, both of which are among the best offered. Toward the end of the meal save room for more than that last sip of wine or a cup of coffee and order one of the superb desserts.

Like any old gentleman, Lubach's can be fussy and crotchety. The service is harried and the food uneven. To ensure an enjoyable evening, come armed with your own celebration—another couple or two—order an early bottle of champagne, and then enjoy the foods they do so well.

Reservations should be made well in advance. It is assumed that a gentleman will be wearing a coat.

2101 North Harbor Dr., San Diego. (714) 232-5129
Mon. - Sat. noon - midnight; closed Sun. & holidays
BA, MC

Little Restaurants of San Diego / 105

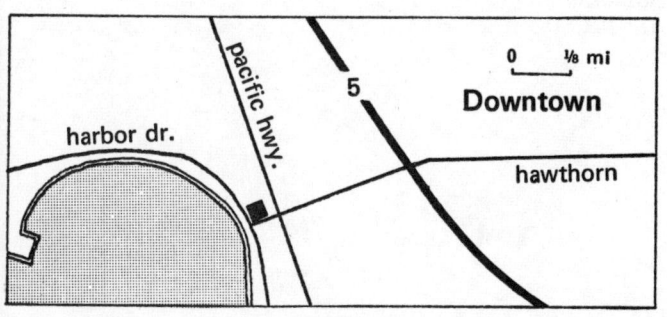

Old Trieste

One of San Diego's best restaurants is hidden away on Morena Blvd. Surrounded by a pizza parlor, apartment buildings, and a freeway, it looks like a neighborhood bar with pretensions of elegance. The classy name and swank 1950s facade do nothing to detract from that general impression. Yet the expensive cars in the lot indicate that the restaurant is somewhat out of place in an area where midnight mechanics ply their trade in a garage across the alley.

To walk inside is to slip back two decades, when a few large, plush booths in a small well-lit room, mostly bare of superfluous decorations, was considered very elegant. And it is elegant here. Nothing looks old, only dated.

The food and service are dated, as well—but delightfully so. The service is unobtrusive but friendly. The food is superb and worth the high prices.

There is no better veal than that served here. Miro's special, a veal scaloppini, is truly great. The cannelloni are excellent, with good filling and fine, subtle pasta. The scampi have a strong shrimp-and-garlic flavor.

There is a little sign on the door requesting that gentlemen wear coats and that women not wear capris. (Even the sign dates itself.) Reservations should be made well in advance—at least a day or so for weekends.

2335 Morena Blvd., San Diego. (714) 276-1841
Tues. - Fri. noon - 2, 5:30 - 10:30; Sat. 5:30 - 10:30;
closed Sun. & Mon.
AE, BA, MC

Old Trieste

moreno
5
clairemont
kane
0
¼ mi
Pacific Beach

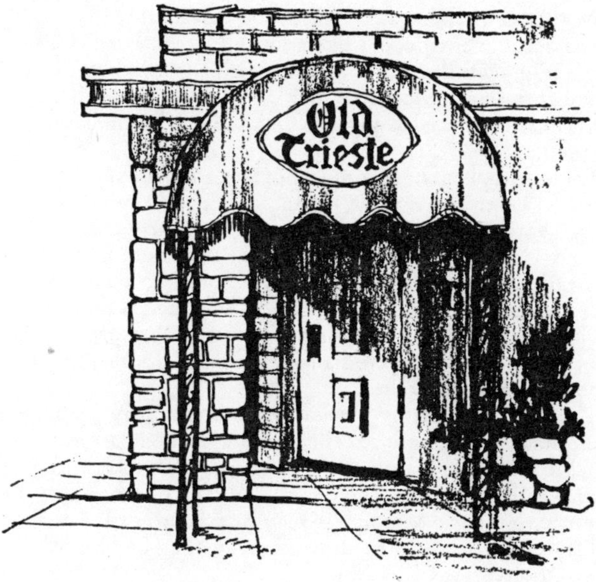

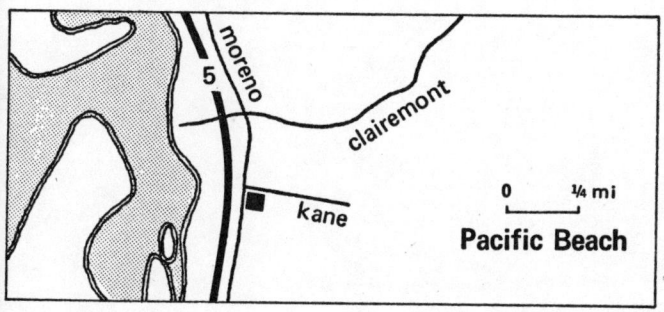

Botsford's Old Place

At this new, elaborately furnished restaurant, the service is as tasteful as the decor: Each course is presented skillfully and gracefully. For example, with the salad comes a chilled fork in a folded linen napkin. Should the knife be removed with the salad plate, a clean one is immediately returned.

These little touches seem important in a restaurant that sets out to convey the feeling of turn-of-the-century dining at its most elegant. Before a table covered with white linen, one sits on an upholstered chair or sofa in a room fit for a railroad financier or an operatic tenor on tour. The walls are creamy white with a subtly antiqued wainscoting; vintage prints and advertisements decorate the space above. The floor is richly carpeted and there is, of course, the indispensible potted palm.

The food is carefully chosen and competently prepared. Both salads offered are excellent, though the heart of romaine is the more unusual. The totuava is moist and flaky. Duck lovers love the duck. The rack of lamb is generous and good—though it may be wise to order it slightly rare, for it can be unnecessarily tough when overdone. Reservations advisable.

Prospect St. at Ivanhoe (upstairs), La Jolla. (714) 459-8262
Sun. 5:30 - 10:30; Mon. - Sat. 6 - 11
BA, MC

Botsfords Old Place

La Jolla

East San Diego

Granger's is a funny little cafe which has been specializing in hamburgers for over 25 years. We used to go there when I was much younger, and on a recent visit I was surprised to find that its operation is still the same. A very large hamburger with fries has been selling for less than a dollar. *(2432 El Cajon Blvd.)*

Azteca sells fast Mexican food here, as well as in a few other parts of the city. Its rolled taco with guacamole is good and not at all expensive. The tostada or bean burrito is good, also. *(5815 El Cajon Blvd.)*

Adams Ave. seems to be spurning antique stores in favor of Mexican food. The fastest place is **Gordo's**. It has good food to go as well as a couple of tables of eating there. *(3332 Adams Ave.)*

Ponce's in Kensington serves lunch. It also serves a convenient early dinner for those making the twilight hour at the Ken Theater. *(4050 Adams Ave.)*

Down in Mission Valley is a favorite sandwich shop called **Lena's**. The sandwiches are made on long Italian rolls. You can order a regular, jumbo, big-footer, or big L; the price varies accordingly. A whole loaf with the works used to come to $3. Lettuce and mayonnaise is one reason why its food is so popular. *(6115 Mission Gorge Rd.)*

Many of the East San Diego restaurants described elsewhere in this book also serve lunch. At **Blumer's** you can get a kosher sandwich, **Nicolosi's** offers Italian sandwiches, and **The Prophet** specializes in the vegetarian variety. The **Sombrero's** memorable taco makes a good lunch.

Hillcrest and Balboa Park

In the heart of the business district there is **Zolezzi's**, which offers Italian tasties along with inexpensive beer and wine.

Also in that area is the **Chicken Pie Shop**. It does not have the atmosphere of Zolezzi's, but it does have good chicken pies. They are inexpensive and filling, especially when accompanied by a huge mound of mashed potatoes and gravy. The chicken sandwiches are nice—a lot like mom used to make, with chunks of chicken in between two pieces of supermarket bread. It also stays open late enough to make a chicken pie dinner possible. *(3801 Fifth Ave. at Robinson.)*

Further down the avenue towards the park are two smaller places catering primarily to the office workers in the area. At **w'Right Fancy Sandwiches** one can get a super sandwich, with fresh fruit and most anything to drink. It might be slightly overpriced, but it offers a great selection of the best quality and quantity in the area. *(3000 Fifth Ave.)*

Just off of Laurel Street is the **Lunch Box Deli**. It has sandwiches but its specialty seems to be a great cheeseburger. On a cold day its chili can't be beat. Around noon comes the businessmen's rush, which creates a line and a few minutes' delay. *(2473 Fifth Ave.)*

Old Town

El Indio is not in Old Town proper, but it is close. It is not actually a restaurant, either, but the best fast-food establishment in the city. There are tables across the street in an island in the intersection. In that respect it is like eating on the Ramblas in Barcelona, where the tables are midstreet and the waiters dash between cars to fetch food and drink. At El Indio's counter efficient girls take your order. The food is cooked fresh and is ready to be picked up a few minutes later. The meat-and-cheese burrito is a big favorite. The taco is good, too. Around noon the place can be busy enough to cause waits as long as 15 minutes. *(3695 India St., near the base of Washington St.)*

The **Old Town Tamale Factory** is two blocks from the new Old Town. It is respectable-looking now with its newly remodeled building. It has good burritos, rivaling El Indio's, at a higher price. *(4263 Taylor St.)*

Eating in the vicinity of the Bazaar del Mundo can be hazardous. For a midmorning snack or a dessert, the **Panderia** in the bazaar has Mexican rolls and sweets.

Casa de Pico is moderately priced for a restaurant in that area. We tried its cheese crisp special and found it to be unique and—had it been cooked fresh—excellent. Over a crisp tortilla, cheese is melted; over that go chunks of beef and slices of tomato and avocado, and a large spoonful of guacamole ends up in the center. (At the rear of the Bazaar del Mundo; the official address is *2754 Calhoun.*)

Just outside the bazaar is **La Casa Blanca**. The food is reasonable but what we tried was not that special. Up the street is **Manuel's**, which serves the most expensive Mexican food in town. For some reason it did not double the price of its tostada, which was pretty good. *(2616 San Diego Ave.)*

Downtown

It is easier than ever to grab a fast, good lunch downtown. These are sandwich shops now, like the **Big Cheese** *(4th and C sts.)*

A good Italian sandwich can be bought at **Guiseppi's**. There are all kinds, but the meatball topped with cheese is recommended. If you have to eat during the lunch rush, call first to place your order. Closes at 2:30 p.m. *(865 7th Ave.; phone; 235-8451.)*

The **House of Nutrition** conceals a little vegetarian cafeteria. It is mostly patronized by thin businesswomen, but that should not deter you. A lunch for a dollar or less is easily done. *(1125 6th Ave.)*

If you want something more substantial, try **La Fonda**. It is basically a bar which at mealtimes becomes a busy restaurant. If the booths are full, simply belly up to the bar and order from there. A daily lunch special, such as two enchiladas, beans, and rice, is about $1.50. There is a good chile relleno and the guacamole salad with chips looks great. *(740 Broadway.)*

At the **Golden Ox** one can order German food for lunch. The wurst sandwiches are only a dollar. More elaborate lunches are also available. *(801 C St.)*

Southeast San Diego

La Mexicana does not look like much from the outside. The interior looks like a Mexican delicatessen-cafe—with soda pop on one side; a deli case with cheese, chorizo, and the like to the front; a counter littered with little things; and a few tables and chairs. The only sound is a light patting coming from the back room behind the deli case. Beyond that door a few women can be seen making tortillas by hand from stone mortars. Most of the food is good. However, the taco in particular is fantastic and cheap. Made from a very fresh, thick handmade corn tortilla, it is filled with shredded beef, lettuce, and a tomato bit or two; and cheese is sprinkled over the top. It is brought from the kitchen too hot to eat and too good to describe. *(2181 Logan St.)*

Chuey's has a good taco, also. It is made with more meat but is much more expensive. Chuey's has the advantage of being a cafe with booths, tables, and extremely cheerful waitresses. The burritos are good also. They are filled with chunks of shredded beef and covered with a slow-burning, earthy, chile-spiced sauce. Beer has been only $.25 for a fair-sized mug. It is the only green quonset hut at the corner of Crosby and Main streets. Parking in the rear.

From Highway 5 take the Crosby exit for both restaurants. Then left on Logan for La Mexicana, straight down Crosby for Chuey's.

The Beaches

In Mission Beach The Crepe Shop serves a mean omelette for about a dollar and a half. Besides ham and cheese and a few others, there is a great spinach omelette. With each is served a honey or marmalade crepe. Since the honey tends to run into the omelette, it would be a good idea to ask for a separate plate. After noon the shop serves only crepes. *(3795 Mission Blvd.)*

For a more leisurely meal than its cafeteria-style service can provide at night, try World Famous in Pacific Beach. During the morning and lunch hours the menu features omelettes, from basic omelettes to an abalone omelette. Each is served with chile sauce, refried beans, and two tortillas. Price varies from under to over $2. (If you prefer such food as omelettes straight, you may want to ask for the sauce to be served on the side.) The best thing about World Famous is the setting, which makes it one of the most delightful brunch places in San Diego. Its windows afford a fine view of the beach, the sunbathers, and the passersby. The wait might be long on a weekend, so some surreptitious sipping can be done in the meantime. *(701 Thomas.)*

If you would like a fish lunch close to Sea World, **Sportsman's Sea Foods** is a possibility. It has seafood cocktails, fish and chips, clams and chips, and a nice fish sandwich on a roll that looks homemade. The prices are not cheap, just reasonable. Open from 11 to 6, except Mondays. (It is located at the Islandia Hotel turnoff, just off West Mission Beach Blvd.)

In La Jolla, the Cafe Renoir is a very pleasant lunch spot. Potted trees, flowers, wall sketches, and the spaciousness of the room make for a refreshing atmosphere. The sandwiches and salads look good. The hot lunch should be avoided. *(912 Silverado, La Jolla.)* Under the same ownership is the **Cafe Lautrec**, which also has a fine luncheon menu.

The Bratskellar has a great view of the cove and decent sandwiches and wine (see page 40).

Coronado

At the **Old Time Shoppe** one can get inexpensive sandwiches or a cheese, meat, and bread platter. The Shoppe is actually an antique store, behind which is a patio with a few tables. The waiter must make his way up and down the stairs of an adjoining building where the kitchen is hidden. Despite this handicap the service remains friendly. In the afternoon there is classical music on the radio. At no time, however, is there wine. The food is put together nicely and served in an attractive fashion. The cold cuts tend to be ho-hum, the kind you might pick up at any supermarket. The cheeses, on the other hand, are quite interesting. *(1113 Orange, Coronado.)*

For a fast snack, try **S & M Submarine Sandwiches, Inc.** The specialty there is a torpedo made on a long Italian roll, with lots of shredded lettuce, a couple of thin tomato slices, and meat of your choice. About a dollar. *(1025 Orange, Coronado.)*

Specialty Food Shops

by Karen Wagstaff

Finding a new bakery, delicatessen or market is, for some, like meeting a new friend. One searches politely in hopes of finding a shared interest or a common passion. Once found, a new and lasting friendship can be made and sealed within moments.

For those adventuresome spirits who always have their ears to the pavement in this search, here are a few new friends we have discovered which you might also enjoy.

BREADS, PASTRIES, TORTILLAS, ETC.

Blumer's Bakery has one of the widest selections of breads and rolls in the city and features one particular kind of bread each day. Its employees are especially proud of their rye breads and bagels. Blumer's also has a delicious and rather international pastry selection, everything from poppy-seed cakes to Danish custards. Prices are fair, considering the quality.

If you are in the market for interesting rolls and breads, try Salerno's Italian Bakery. There you can buy a special turtle roll that is an exact replica and could end up being the talk of your party. Kaiser rolls, French rolls and assorted breads are also available. In addition, Salerno's sells some gorgeous Italian pastries that tend to make one's eyes bigger than one's stomach. *(3102 University Ave.)*

Thanks to Bagel World, San Diego is well provided with an infinite variety of this famous roll. Bagel World not only distributes to most of the major delicatessens in town, it also sells retail at its one location. *(6323 El Cajon Blvd.)*

Ross Sands also has a fine variety of specialty rolls. Its selection of bagels is very extensive, featuring egg, water, whole-wheat, and sesame seed—compliments of Bagel World. *(Rosecrans and Midway, Point Loma.)*

Should you want to feed an army on one loaf of bread, you can order a ten-pound (!) sourdough loaf at **Golden West Market**. Give the place three days' notice and then go pick up your large-sized baby. *(7907 Cajon Rd., El Cajon.)*

Fresh homemade Arab or Bible bread, a newfound favorite for many, can be picked up fresh at the **Middle Eastern Gourmet**. The white loaves are made each day; whole-wheat must be ordered specially. *(1901 El Cajon Blvd.)*

La Mexicana makes hand-made, homemade corn and flour tortillas to order. They are thick, warm, super-fresh, and cheap. *(2181 Logan St., National City.)*

For fresh factory-made tortillas, try **La Mesa Food Products**. It also sells taco shells, tortilla chips, and bunelos. Prepared empanadas, tamales, enchiladas, and taco meat can be purchased as well. *(8328 Center Dr., La Mesa.)*

For a tortilla of a different sort, **Woo Chee Chong's** Oriental market sells packaged won ton and egg roll skins by the pound. *(633 16th St.)*

For delicious pastries and pies, **Gloor's** has been a favorite of many for years. It is a small shop, but of course we all know that the best things come from small places. *(4090 Adams Blvd.)*

Margaret's has made its reputation on its pies. Although the place is primarily a restaurant, you can buy pies to take out. If it's a fruit pie, the filling is sure to be of the fresh rather than the canned variety. All are homemade. *(5952 Severin Dr., La Mesa.)*

Panderia Nacional Bakery specializes in Mexican pastries and breads. If you are a connoisseur of such delights, another choice, (not to be confused) is the Panaderia in Old Town. There, among other things, you can buy the popular churros, which is dough that has been pressed through a long tubular mold and fried. Each one is well over a foot long and especially good with coffee or cocoa. *(Panderia Nacional Bakery, 1701 National Ave.; Panaderia, Bazaar Del Mundo, Old Town.)*

Harvey's bakery allows you not only to choose a delectable treat but also the opportunity to sit right down and enjoy it. There's an interesting display of pastries, cakes, and breads, and it's a nice place to rest your feet. *(328 3rd St., Chula Vista.)*

For a really special occasion, the **Grove Pastry Shop** will bake a cake you won't forget: layer upon layer with assorted preserves in between and a fabulous whipped-cream frosting. Call well ahead to order the exact size desired. *(7815 Broadway, Lemon Grove. 466-1974).*

One can also obtain a cake frosted in whipped cream from **George's Wonderful World of Cakes**. George's has cakes galore—all sizes, colors, and flavors. His lemon snow cake is famous as are his fresh strawberry pies (when in season). *(1519 Highland Ave., National City.)*

MEATS

Sausage King has a fabulous variety of cold German-style sausages, wursts, etc., and carries a wide selection of fresh veal, from chops to roasts, in the regular meat section. Homemade pretzels and hard continental rolls are also for sale. *(811 W. Washington St.; 319 3rd St., Chula Vista; 7097 University Ave., La Mesa.)*

Golden West Market sells Italian sausages. They are handmade, lean, and come both spicy and regular. *(7907 Cajon Rd., El Cajon.)*

Chorizo (Mexican-style sausage), both pork and beef, can be found at **La Mexicana**, along with pickled pigs' feet and crisply fried pork rind. *(2181 Logan St., National City.)*

Farmers Market in the Bazaar Del Mundo, Old Town, has a very large selection of both domestic and imported cold meats at reasonable prices, in addition to an impressive display of cheeses. *(2754 Calhoun, Old Town.)*

Woo Chee Chong's meat counter can be a real education. There are fresh innards like tripe and sheep kidneys. Live crab can be selected, as can several sizes of shrimp. Fresh pigs' feet, pigs' tails, octopus, and squid (both frozen) can also be found. For the exotic and the unusual, this is the place. *(633 16th St.)*

You can buy a delicious homemade chicken pie at the **Chicken Pie Shop**. Hot and crusty or unbaked and ready for the freezer and baking at home, they are amazingly inexpensive. *(3801 Fifth Ave., Hillcrest).*

FRESH PRODUCE

If you are looking for vegetables at vegetable-stand prices, try the Farmers Market in Old Town. It offers a good selection for such a small place, and most of the prices are small as well. The vegetables look locally grown. *(2754 Calhoun, Old Town.)*

Woo Chee Chong's produce section yields such exotic items as a string-bean variety called Sitow that measures well over a foot in length. You can also find unusual melons, obscure greens, snow peas, etc. *(633 16th St.)*

The House of Produce deals with locally grown vegetables and fruits. Although they aren't always picture-perfect, they are usually good and fresh. Also available are farm-fresh brown eggs and raw milk. *(1258 Broadway, El Cajon.)*

SPECIALTY MARKETS

While in Filippi's delicatessen and pizza house, I came upon the largest jar of marinated artichoke hearts I'd ever seen. It was difficult to tear myself away from that to notice the huge selection of canned goods, olive oils, and pastas. If you can get past the artichokes, perhaps some even better treats can be found. In the same neighborhood are many other small shops dealing in Italian foods. *(1747 India St.)*

Oriental and Filipino food items such as egg noodles, shrimp chips, frozen limpia, and Filipino sausage can be found at Javiera's Orientex. *(211 Highland Ave, National City)*

Another little Oriental food shop is the Kyoto Gift and Food store. You can get fresh tofu there when it can't be found elsewhere. Call for delivery dates. *(2303 Highland Ave, National City.)*

More conveniently located, perhaps, is Osaka Oriental Foods. It carries many exotic and unusual items. *(3645 University Ave.)*

ICE CREAM

There are three ice cream parlors around town which sell homemade-style ice cream. The flavors are genuine, made from real fruit whenever possible. Only one or two of the flavors are sweetened with honey, because the taste of honey spoils most ice cream. (One owner assured us that he uses the same type of sweetening base as does the dairy that claims to use only honey.) The parlors are Niederfrank's, *(726 A St., National City);* the Ice Cream Factory, *(4421 Genessee, Clairemont);* and Father Nature, *(Cape May, Ocean Beach).*

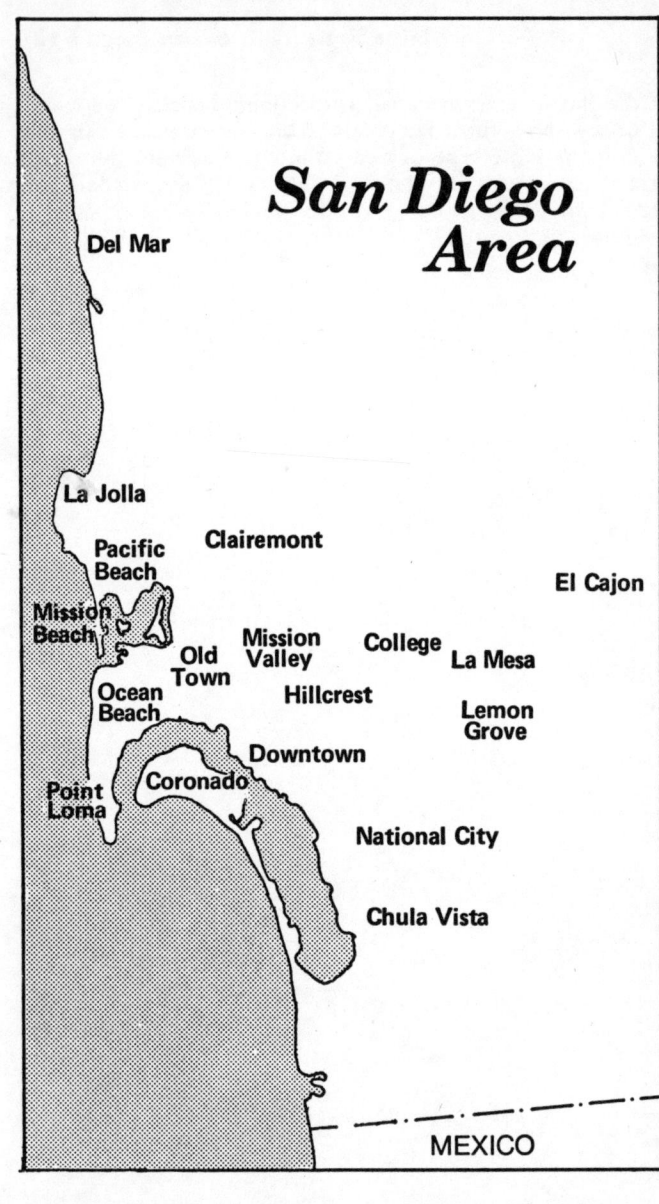

Restaurants by Region

CHULA VISTA
Harvey's	118
Ocean Fresh Seafood Cafe	88
Sausage King	119

CLAIREMONT
Ice Cream Factory	121

COLLEGE
Aspen Mine Co.	98
College Restaurant	10
New Moon	26

CORONADO
Old Time Shoppe	116
S & M Submarine Sandwiches, Inc.	116

DEL MAR
Rosendo's Hideaway	76

DOWNTOWN
Anthony's Star of the Sea	96
Antoine's Sheik	66
Big Cheese	113
Filippi's	120
Golden Ox	113
Guiseppi's	113
Hob Nob Hill	12
House of Nutrition	113
La Fonda	113
Lubach's	104
Miki-San	62
Old Spaghetti Factory	60
Tom Lai's	80
Woo Chee Chong's	118

EAST SAN DIEGO
Azteca	110
Bagel World	117
Bea's Rancho Chico	72
Blumer's Bakery	64
Gloor's	118
Gordo's	110
Granger's	110
Lena's	110
Middle Eastern Gourmet	118
Nicolosi's	54
Osaka Oriental Foods	120
Ponce's	110
Prophet	48
Three Mermaids	78
Venice	56

EL CAJON
DeAngelis	50
Golden West Market	118
House of Produce	120
Pinnacle Peak	18

HILLCREST/BALBOA PARK
Black Forest Inn	40
Chicken Pie Shop	111
Lunch Box Deli	111
w'Right Fancy Sandwiches	111
Zolezzi's	58

LA JOLLA
Alfonso's Hideaway	68
Botsford's Old Place	108
Bratskellar	42
Cafe Lautrec	38

Cafe Renoir	115
Chart House	100
Chez Francois	102
Gatekeeper	46
Restaurant Madrid	94
Schnitzelbank	44

LA MESA
La Mesa Food Products	118
Margaret's	118

LEMON GROVE
Grove Pastry Shop	119

MIDWAY
China Land	24
Lourdes	34
Nordic Inn	92

MISSION BEACH
Crepe Shop	32
Saska's	·20
Sportsman's Seafoods	115

MISSION VALLEY
First Edition	14
Kelly's	16

NATIONAL CITY
El Juan's Cafe	74
George's Wonderful World of Cakes	119
Javiera's Orientex	120
John Bull	22
Kyoto Gift and Food	120
La Mexicana	114
Niederfrank's	120
Sampaquita	36

NORTH PARK
Salerno's Italian Bakery	117

OCEAN BEACH
Father Nature	121
Thee Bungalow	28

OLD TOWN
Casa de Pico	112
El Indio	112
Farmer's Market	119
La Casa Blanca	112
Manuel's	112
Old Town Tamale Factory	112

PANDERIA
Panaderia Nacional Bakery	118

PACIFIC BEACH
Aljones	70
Fish Place	84
Greenery	30
Giulio's	52
Krishna Mulvaney	86
Old Trieste	106
World Famous	90

POINT LOMA
Fishermen's Wharf Grotto	82
Ross Sands	117

SOUTHEAST SAN DIEGO
Chuey's	114

Alphabetical Index

Alfonso's Hideaway	68	Fishermen's Wharf Grotto	82
Aljones	70	Fish Place	84
Anthony's Star of the Sea	96	Gatekeeper	46
Antoine's Sheik	66	George's Wonderful World of Cakes	119
Aspen Mine Co.	98	Giulio's	52
Azteca	110	Gloor's	118
Bagel World	117	Golden Ox	113
Bea's Rancho Chico	72	Golden West Market	118
Big Cheese	113	Gordo's	110
Black Forest Inn	40	Granger's	110
Blumer's Bakery	64	Greenery	30
Botsford's Old Place	108	Grove Pastry Shop	119
Bratskellar	42	Guiseppi's	113
Cafe Lautrec	38	Harvey's	118
Cafe Renoir	115	Hob Nob Hill	12
Casa de Pico	112	House of Nutrition	113
Chart House	100	House of Produce	120
Chez Francois	102	Ice Cream Factory	121
Chicken Pie Shop	111	Javiera's Orientex	120
China Land	24	John Bull	22
Chuey's	114	Kelly's	16
College Restaurant	10	Krishna Mulvaney	86
Crepe Shop	32	Kyoto Gift and Food	120
DeAngelis	50	La Casa Blanca	112
El Indio	112	La Fonda	113
El Juan's Cafe	74	La Mesa Food Products	118
Farmer's Market	119	La Mexicana	114
Father Nature	121	Lena's	110
Filippi's	120	Lourdes	34
First Edition	14		

Lubach's	104	Ponce's	110
Lunch Box Deli	111	Prophet	48
Manuel's	112	Restaurant Madrid	94
Margaret's	118	Rosendo's Hideaway	76
Middle Eastern Gourmet	118	Ross Sands	117
Miki-San	62	Salerno's Italian Bakery	117
New Moon	26	Sampaquita	36
Nicolosi's	54	S & M Submarine Sandwiches, Inc.	116
Niederfrank's	120	Saska's	20
Nordic Inn	92	Sausage King	119
Ocean Fresh Seafood Cafe	88	Schnitzelbank	44
Old Spaghetti Factory	60	Sportsman's Seafoods	115
Old Time Shoppe	116	Thee Bungalow	28
Old Town Tamale Factory	112	Three Mermaids	78
Old Trieste	106	Tom Lai's	80
		Venice	56
Osaka Oriental Foods	120	Woo Chee Chong's	118
Panaderia Nacional Bakery	118	World Famous	90
Panaderia	118	w'Right Fancy Sandwiches	111
Pinnacle Peak	18	Zolezzi's	58

After Hours

The streets in town do not roll up at midnight, just the restaurants. A hamburger from a box may not be what you are looking for, but often it is the only kind of food quickly found. There are a few restaurants, however, that do keep later hours. Here are some:

Daily

Chinese Food	China Land (3:30 a.m.)
Hamburgers	Saska's (3 a.m.)
Sandwiches	Bratskellar (2 a.m., except Sun.)
Filipino Food	Sampaquita (2 a.m.), Lourdes (midnight)
Mexican Food	Bea's (midnight Monday–Thursday, 3 a.m. Friday & Saturday)
Italian Sandwiches	Nicolosi's (midnight weeknights, 2 a.m. Friday & Saturday)
Steaks	Kelley's (11:45 p.m.)

Weekends Only

Onion Soup	The First Edition (1 a.m.)
Beef and Crab	The Aspen Mine Co. (12:45 a.m.)

Other ♡ Camaro Guides

All beautifully illustrated with maps and sketches

... For your low cost dining pleasure, plus a few splurges.

☐ Hidden Restaurants: Northern California
☐ Hidden Restaurants: Southern California
☐ Little Restaurants of Los Angeles
☐ Little Restaurants of San Francisco
☐ Little Restaurants of San Diego

... Or for just a bit of adventure throughout the California Countryside.

☐ Wine Tasting in California: A Free Weekend
☐ L.A. On Foot: A Free Afternoon

TO: Camaro Publishing Co.
P. O. Box 90430
Los Angeles, California 90009

Please send the books checked above. Enclosed is $ _____ which includes $1.95 per book ordered, plus 6% tax and 25¢ postage/handling.

Name _____

Address _____

City _____ State _____ Zip _____

☐ Check here to include your name on the mailing list for new announcements of Camaro's Adventure Guides.

A Special Notice to our readers:

Excellence is our publishing aim—to provide the best, most accurate and timely information in the world about travel/adventure, good food and wine, all at the very lowest prices. We have discovered that you don't have to spend a fortune to enjoy dining out or travel. You just have to know where to go.

To speed making our latest information available to the adventurous, we have just started the Newwest California Club which will present monthly, the very latest of the very best. . .and all for not much money. Try it and see

---

Newwest California Club Membership

Mail To: Secretary, Newwest California Club
P.O. Box 90430, Los Angeles, Ca., 90009

$3.00 per year or special charter subscription: $6.00 for three years, or $25 for lifetime Gold Circle membership.

Membership includes subscription to NEWWEST.

New Member:

Name_____

Street_____

City, State, Zip_____

Enclosed $_____

FREE Dinner for Two

If you think we've made some blatant omissions in our selections, please send us the name of your favorite restaurant not mentioned in a Camaro Guide. Every other month we'll draw a card, you could win a free dinner for two at a restaurant in your area of California. It's worth a try, just tear out this postcard and drop it in the mail.

Name of Restaurant: _____

Address: _____

Phone #: _____

Type of food served: _____

_____

Price range for dinners: _____

Your favorite dish: _____

_____

Other comments: _____

_____

Your name: _____

Your address: _____

_____

Any comments on the book: _____

_____

CAMARO PUBLISHING COMPANY
P.O. Box 90430
Los Angeles, California
90009